PRESENTING PAULINE

PRESENTING PAULINE

A memoir by
Pauline Fraser

I was a dancer

as told to
LOUISE BRASS

Outskirts Press, Inc.
Denver, Colorado

*This book is dedicated to
Rex, Teresa and Ryan*

Acknowledgments

Our grateful thanks to

Anthony Brass
editing

Sheila and Ron Blanch
fact checking

The Plymouth City Museum and Art Gallery
for very kind assistance

and to

Daughters of the British Empire USA
for many cups of tea during the
creation of this work.

Contents

CHAPTER 1

Presenting Pauline

D arkness.

Then came the sound of enemy bombers overhead.

I felt my mother shaking me, trying to wake me up.

"Wake up, Pauline! Wake up! We're being bombed!"

I didn't want to wake up. I'd been performing at the theater until late the night before. Now it was only 3 a.m.

My body ached. My limbs wanted rest. But my common sense told me I had to get up or risk being blown to bits.

I could hear the air raid wardens outside of our block of flats, yelling for people to run quickly to their shelters. The Luftwaffe was overhead and dropping bombs all over London.

We threw on our dressing gowns, grabbed a couple of pillows and hurried down the stairs. The nearest shelter was in an underground nightclub. That's where we headed.

With our slippers on our feet and our hair still in curlers, we weren't the only ones. Other people, equally surprised by the night raid, were rushing beside us toward Café de Paris. We squashed into the elevator and were quickly propelled many floors down to the safety of the underground club.

When the elevator doors opened, we were shocked to walk right into the club and see people all dressed up in elegant eveningwear.

They were on the floor dancing, others were dining, and here we stood, very embarrassed in our nightclothes with no make up on to help make us look even remotely presentable.

The club manager immediately came up to us.

"What on earth's going on?" he demanded.

"Here's our passes," I said. "This is where we are supposed to come when there's an air raid," I explained, thanking my lucky stars that I had remembered to grab the passes as we'd hurried out of our flat.

Everyone had a designated shelter to go to during the war, when an air raid started. The club seemed completely unprepared though, and the manager didn't know what to do with us. He spotted some vacant tables, and, ushering us over to them he encouraged us to sit down quickly.

While we tried to look invisible, he ordered the waiters to bring us cups of tea and sandwiches. Everyone was staring at us. We didn't know where to look.

But we felt sure we would be all right here—deep underground—safe from the devastation that was occurring over our heads.

By daybreak, the German bombers had depleted their

deadly ordinance, and we were told we could go back to our homes—if the buildings were still standing—and we could get a few hours of sleep.

I found out later that we shouldn't have been at Café de Paris at all. The nightclub wasn't a shelter. There was a mistake on the locations printed on some air raid passes. Our designated shelter was actually in the basement of Russell's Department Store.

What I also didn't know at the time was that while the Café de Paris was safe on this night, it was to become one of the bloodiest scenes of devastation in the city of London during all of World War II.

I was a young revue artist then, and was also working as a model for magazine ads, and as a film extra.

I have to confess that I faked my age during the 1930s and 1940s. It's what you needed to do in those days to perform on the stage and to make films, if you were under the legal age. I'll explain why as my story unfolds.

Was it worth it?

Oh, yes!

The stage performances, films, advertising gigs, cabaret shows and pantomime appearances kept my mother and me alive through The Depression of the 1930s, through my Hollywood adventures as a teenager, and through the London Blitz as a young woman.

And my tap dancing, singing—and perhaps I should also humbly admit my school girl figure—won me a spot as a glamorous Windmill Girl, and a place at the table with princes, spies, and other powerful men and women.

Yes, I played with the rich and famous.

I lunched with Gen. George Patton and slept in Maj. Gen. Jimmy Doolittle's bed—that wasn't planned of course—and Doolittle wasn't there at the time. It happened one night at the general's wartime headquarters in High Wickham, when he was in London, preparing for the invasion of Europe.

It's all true to the best of my memory.

There is so much to tell. They say the best place to start is at the beginning.

I was born in my aunt's house in Grantham, England on a humid August day, when the Roaring '20s were in full swing.

A river ran around the edge of the back garden. There were no fairies at the bottom of that garden when I was born, because a 100-year flood had covered half the back lawn and was approaching the house.

My mother, Louisa, was screeching as she gave birth to me in the front bedroom on the second floor of the large home. It was the room where all my cousins had also been born.

My mother, who was thirty-five years old at the time, was screaming her head off. So the doctor gave her a good dose of chloroform and I came into the world half asleep; it took them some time to wake me up.

I was reminded of that, years later, when I was performing with a theater group. We had a session where we described how we viewed each other, and how we each came across to an audience. One girl said, "Pauline always has a dreaming look about her."

I told her it was because my mother was given chloroform as I was being born. In the 1920s, when women's birth pangs became almost unbearable, the doctors would give them chloroform.

In my case it must have been okay, because I did make it into the world, and my mother survived.

Here I was, Pauline Mabbett, destined to become deathly sick with scarlet fever at age four, yet destined also to survive and make fleeting appearances in Alfred Hitchcock's film, *Sabotage*; I'm the child in the white beret. I also had a speaking part in the horror flick, *Night Must Fall*.

I am thankful that I would also become strong enough to tap dance my way through World War II in London theaters and clubs, frantically changing costumes, while dodging Luftwaffe bombing raids.

My father, Orlando Mabbett, wasn't in Grantham when I was born. He was in Birmingham on tour as the musical director of the Carl Rosa Opera Company. The company was famous for presenting the first ever performance of Puccini's *La Boheme* in Britain. In the late 1800s, the opera company also performed for Queen Victoria at Balmoral Castle. By the early 1900s, Carl Rosa Opera Company was known as a permanent English institution.

On the night I was born, my father was in Manchester conducting the orchestra.

My mother dispatched a telegram to inform him he had a daughter. To celebrate, he ordered champagne for the whole company after the show.

My mother was furious at such an extravagance, because he hadn't sent any money home for a long time and it had been a struggle for her.

My father was a child prodigy. At age 12 he started playing in an orchestra. In fact, even at that young age, he played first violin for the Birmingham Orchestra conducted by his father, my grandfather.

My father, who also played the viola and the piano like a virtuoso, could speak French and German fluently. He was a very brilliant man—a very clever musician. One of his greatest triumphs was when he conducted *The Miracle*, written by the German composer, Karl Vollmoller, in 1912. Lady Diana Manners played the principal part of Madonna in the Birmingham production of the opera.

During World War II my father came in and out of my life. My mother never saw him after the war. She didn't know what happened to him.

* * *

We stayed with my grandmother in Grantham until I was three years old. Then, our lives changed when my grandmother was taken ill. On her deathbed, (mother told me) grandmother said that she would leave money to mother's two sisters, but she would leave the house to my mother.

Grandmother wanted to know what my mother's plans were.

"We should probably stay here and live in this house," my mother told her.

"Oh, no you can't possibly do that. You must sell the house," grandmother said.

"Why?" asked my mother, surprised.

"You have to think about Pauline's career," was grandmother's reply.

Because I was only three years old at the time, my mother hadn't given my career much thought.

"You must go to London, because Pauline is going to go into the theater. That's where you have to be. This is no place for her to start," my grandmother said.

How she knew that I was to go on the stage, we could hardly imagine.

After my grandmother's death, my mother sold the house in Grantham, and off we went to London, which was a very different place from what it is now.

Fortunately, mother found a job as assistant manageress of the bars at Daly's Theatre. Each bar was located at a different level. Two bars were downstairs in the stalls, one was at the dress circle level, one was in the upper circle and one bar was in the gallery. It was a big responsibility.

People rushed to the bars for a quick drink, during the interval of the show. If the show was boring they stayed at the bar.

At the age of four I became seriously ill with scarlet fever. In those days you lived or you died. There was no cure for the contagious disease that produced a horrible red eruption. So I was immediately sent to a fever hospital, where I spent three months. I was very sick and very miserable.

Naturally, we weren't allowed any visitors of any kind, because of the danger of contagion. But my mother used to come almost every day. The nurses would allow her to look at me through a window. Sometimes though, she would be allowed to approach my bedside.

The reason my mother was allowed to approach the bed was because she would bribe the nurses with theater tickets. She was a very welcome visitor.

Eventually, I was transferred to the hospital nursing home for another month.

When my mother came to pick me up and take me home, she hardly recognized me; I was so thin. They had chopped off most of my hair and put me in a striped calico dress.

I was humiliated.

As always with children when they are ill, the case was to send them into the countryside to recuperate. So I went back to Grantham to live with my Aunty Ann Levick.

Her husband had a successful business. He owned a garage, and sold cars and motorbikes. Uncle Will Levick fixed cars, had a showroom, and sold petrol (gasoline as it's called in the United States). He had two gas pumps in front of the business.

One of his good customers at Levick's Garage was a Mr. Roberts. He had a grocery store at the end of the road called North Parade, just a couple of blocks from Levick's Garage. The great North Parade was a major road that ran between London and Scotland.

My aunt would buy groceries from Roberts' Grocery Shop on a regular basis and I would go with her and play with Mr. and Mrs. Roberts' eldest daughter, Margaret. She was about four at the time, and destined to be world famous.

I was slightly older than Margaret. She would be playing

in the shop, and I would often join her, while my aunt and Mrs. Roberts discussed various affairs that were going on in our small Lincolnshire town.

Margaret and I would sit in the corner of the store chatting. She was a very bright little girl. She was so bright that she eventually became famous and is still referred to as "The Iron Lady."

When she grew up she married Dennis Thatcher, and she was elected the country's first woman prime minister. Queen Elizabeth II eventually made Margaret Thatcher a Dame, which is a title of honor. As prime minister, she was greatly respected throughout the free world, and was feared behind the Iron Curtain and the Bamboo Curtain.

My cousins attended Kesteven School with Margaret Thatcher, in Grantham, and they told me a few stories about their school days. After they graduated, one of my cousins went back for a school reunion and asked a teacher about her most recent class.

"Oh, we had a great year, except … one girl was so mouthy," the teacher replied. "She was always opinionated. I don't know what's going to become of her!"

That "mouthy" girl went on to do great things as a prime minister of Great Britain.

While I was in Grantham, my mother found a small flat in London on Charing Cross Road, close to Piccadilly, and the theaters. It was beneficial for my father too because that's where they had the musician's union. He went to the union hall regularly to find out what company he would be touring with next.

One day my other uncle, Alec Russell, suggested to my mother that maybe I should attend a boarding school near Grantham. It was very expensive, but he felt that I would get an education there.

Sleaford School for Girls was in the countryside. So, my mother thought it would be very good for my health—better for me than being in London. She almost had a fit, though, when she realized what the cost would be for the school uniforms and books, etc. She almost changed her mind.

But unfortunately, the plan went ahead and I was shipped off to the boarding school.

At age five, I was the youngest boarder there and consequently mostly ignored; I was very unhappy.

Although that area of England is very pretty—albeit rather flat—I hated being at the school. All I wanted was to go home to London.

CHAPTER 2

The Escape to London

I spent about 18 miserable months at the boarding school. Fortunately, one day my mother met an old friend of hers in Piccadilly, named Lucy Monks. She was also a mother with a son about my age. Lucy had her little boy with her and my mother was interested in what they were doing.

"My husband is a steward on the White Star and Cunard lines' ships most of the time," Lucy said. "He goes between Southampton and India and is away a great deal of the time. So we are busy filming."

They were members of the Film Artists Association. Lucy and her little boy were both registered with the association. They each were getting paid a guinea a day, that's one pound, one shilling in the old money, and about $2 American today. That was a good day's pay in the 1920s.

So immediately, my mother thought that was a great idea,

and I was yanked out of boarding school as soon as the term ended. We arranged to join the Film Artists Association.

It was very exciting for me to go from boarding school to filming. We paid dues and pretty soon we got a call to go down to one of the studios.

But I was only seven years old, and it was against the law for any child under the age of 14 to work in films. When a filming opportunity came up, my mother used to have to say I was sick that day if I wasn't in school.

I was sick a lot.

My mother would bribe the teachers to mark me present when I was away by giving them theater tickets to different shows. There was no television back then so theater shows were very big, and giving free tickets was a technique that worked time and time again.

By the time I was 8, I was beginning to do advertising work for different products and appearing in various newsletters and on the front of knitting magazines. Also, I started taking a lot of dancing lessons. I took tap and ballet and attended an academy called Terry's.

Miss Terry conducted the classes on Saturday mornings. We had to wear short black satin pants and white blouses. I felt very grown up, and I enjoyed lessons there very much.

She also had a troupe of 12-year-old children who were licensed to go on the stage.

We all had ambitions that when we reached the age of 12, we would go on the stage with Miss Terry's troupe of dancers.

When a promotional job came up, my agent called to say

I was wanted at a studio where they photographed children for birthday cards. The cards were sold in all the Woolworth stores, which were nationwide.

The studio instructed me to come in a Brownie outfit. Most English girls my age were Brownies. But I had to borrow a uniform from another little girl, because by that time I was no longer a Brownie. I was already a Girl Guide.

The verse on the front of the card wished the recipient a happy birthday and many more.

With a little hat that Brownies wear—and the dark brown uniform complete with a few badges—the image of my smiling face traveled all over Britain, and no doubt graced many birthday tables and sideboards of little birthday girls.

For two weeks each summer, when I was still very young, we would get away for summer holidays to the home of some relatives in Eastbourne, on the south coast. The relatives owned a tuck shop in a large house near Eastbourne College. Students would go there to take a break from their studies to buy chocolates, sweets, and other treats, and they would "tuck in," greedily.

Summertime in Eastbourne was always quieter than during the rest of the year, because most of the students went home when school was out in June, July and August. We stayed in one of the extra bedrooms above the tuck shop.

During our visits, my father conducted the orchestra at the Eastbourne Winter Gardens. It was a major form of entertainment for people staying at the boarding houses for their summer holidays. We attended all his shows, and enjoyed the concerts very much.

Most days I played on the pebbly beach with my cousin, Kathleen, who always came with us to the seaside town.

When the tide went out, the ebbing water gave way to long, flat stretches of sand. We would walk out on the wet sand and make sandcastles that shimmered in the sunlight. We decorated them with seaweed and shells, and waited for the tide to come back in.

After a while, the waves would come rolling in all around the sandcastles. The ocean made the miniature buildings collapse almost instantly, and carried what was left of them back into its foamy green depths before our very eyes. We would squeal with delight.

It was as if the sea was playing with us on those carefree, sun-filled, far away days.

* * *

Of course, school was not completely forgotten.

When I was nine, I attended Colebrook School in Islington, a London suburb. Classes convened each day for morning sessions. We wore dark brown tunics and pale lemon blouses. I rather fancied that the uniforms made us look very studious.

One of my first advertising jobs was for Boots the Chemist, a chain of pharmacies as popular to the British as Walgreens or CVS Pharmacy is to folks in the U.S.A. Boots the Chemist shops had branches in almost every town. They wanted me to go down to their factory headquarters in Nottingham, and appear in a film that was designed to teach their personnel how to deal with customers.

Boots paid the train fare for my mother and me to go to Nottingham. They had a mock-up of a chemist shop and a lady was to portray my mother.

I was supposed to go into the "shop" because I needed some pills for constipation. The idea was to show how to make it easy for a child to take medication.

So, off I went into the shop, trying to look constipated. My "mother" finally talked me into taking some laxative pills. I was paid three guineas for that particular job, plus the train fares, which was very nice. Getting paid was important because my father still wasn't really supporting us. He was living at home at that time. Things were difficult; he was successful, but he just didn't realize that he had to support a family.

Then, one day, my mother's work stalled at the theater. The management announced that the theater had to close down for some time, while they prepared for a new show.

You might say, because I was filming and doing advertising work I was the sole supporter of my family, at the age of nine. At last, a new show opened at the theater and my mother could go back to work.

The flats we lived in were called Sandringham Flats, and were only three blocks from Piccadilly, on Charing Cross Road. They were built by Lord Sandringham in the 1880s for London policemen, so it was a very safe place to live. Policemen were coming and going day and night. We had a three-bedroom apartment. It was a bit squashed, but we managed because the location was so wonderful.

One day on a film set, a panic ensued when we learned

that a London County Council inspector was coming to the studio to see if any children were involved with the filming—which we were.

One of the assistant directors rushed onto the set.

"Get these kids out of here quickly," he said. "Take them up to the wardrobe."

We went immediately; we were well-trained. They stuck us into big wardrobe baskets and threw costumes on top of us, and told us to keep quiet and not to say anything.

When the inspector came into the studio he was told: "We don't have any children here. You must have been misinformed. We don't even have any children in this film. It must have been some other studio."

Meanwhile, up in the wardrobe room, we were deathly silent in our hiding places, while the inspector searched for about an hour. On the set, when the director yells, "Quiet on the set!" no one ever moves a hair until he calls, "Action!"

So it was on the day of the inspection.

As soon as the inspector left, we got action all right. All the children were sent home, each clutching their pay of one guinea.

CHAPTER 3

Little Miss Hurricane

An old friend of my mother's, who was in her late 50s, was working on Sunday afternoons in what was called Working Men's Clubs. The clubs were for working class families and usually consisted of one large room with a stage at one end, and naturally, a bar at the other end.

This woman said she would take me along with her if I wanted to do a song and dance on the stage for the children of the families. If I did, she would pay me two and sixpence (about 50 cents).

So we agreed that I would spend my Sundays at the clubs. We went by train, or tram, to the outlying districts where these Working Men's Clubs were, and I would do my little song and tap dance.

I was not only performing live at this time, I was doing publicity work as well.

During weeknights, I would sometimes go with my mother to the theater where she worked. If a box were empty, I would creep in and watch the live shows. Some productions were big musicals with lots of dance numbers; I soaked it all up.

Some of the presentations were plays. Many British plays were produced in London in the 1930s. Others were grand American musical productions. I watched them all from the best seats in the house.

Every big movie house had live shows in between the films. They'd have two big movies and three shows. Of course, you were only allowed to perform in two live shows if you were 12 or 13 years old. If you were 14 or older, you could be in all three live shows per day.

At the age of 12, I was old enough to apply for a license to appear on the legitimate stage. That was cause for celebration. However, we delayed because we were apprehensive about applying to the county council for a license, in case it was known that I was one of the children filming and performing on the stage, while underage. So we were being very cautious.

Either way, it was also cause for many more dance lessons.

There was a dancing school about three blocks from where we lived called Ascot School of Dance. Douglas Ascot, who had a reputation for being a great tap dancer and teacher, ran the school. So my mother took me along to see him; I did a tap routine.

"Oh, no, no," he said. "What I teach is far superior to what your daughter is doing."

So, there was no doubt that I should join his school of dance.

My mother asked what he charged for lessons. When I heard his answer, I thought it was far more than we could afford.

But Dougie, as we called him, had a solution.

"My young daughter is coming up to stay with me and I really can't have her where I live," he said.

I never knew the reason, but I figured his flat was too small for two.

"In return for lessons for Pauline, could she live with you?" he asked my mother.

My mother agreed to the arrangement and his daughter, Margery, came to live with us. She was six months older than me and we went to attend lessons together everyday in the beautiful studio, just a few blocks away on Charing Cross Road.

Later, his younger daughter, Hazel, aged 5, also came to stay with us. She was to become a fantastic tap dancer and eventually was known as England's "Shirley Temple."

Dougie was so enthused with teaching that I'd be there sometimes until nine o'clock at night, and I had to go to school in the morning. Practicing so late wasn't very good. On top of that, I had to really work hard to keep up with his style of dancing.

When Dougie decided to put on a children's tapping act, he chose myself, Margery, and two other young girls who were pupils of his. We were called "The Four Petite Ascots."

There was only one problem: I would have to go and

actually get a license before I could legally perform in public.

Of course, when we went to get the license, the man who issued them refused us.

"Oh no," he said sternly, shaking his head. "Mrs. Mabbett, we know your daughter has been filming for years and breaking the law, and we don't want to issue her a license."

"No, no, no, my daughter never has," my mother insisted.

But he wouldn't give in.

So she made a big noise. She cried. She pounded the desk, and started looking like she was having a stroke. In the end, he agreed that I could have the license, just to shut her up.

"I never, ever want to hear that she is going down to a studio again," he stated.

"Oh, she never has," was the reply.

Putting on a theatrical show is no small thing. We had a big tapping mat to use at each performance. It was rolled up for storing, or while traveling, and then unrolled across the stage before the curtain went up at each performance.

When the curtain rose, we opened the show in little frilly, net dresses and we did a slow tap dance.

We followed our "frilly" opening with Margery doing a solo tap dance, while I frantically changed into a little sailor outfit. As soon as Margery was through, she dashed off the stage and the two other girls came on in sequined costumes, like bathing suits, and did what we called a "shimmy" type of dance. The lights would flicker in different colors on the sequins while they danced.

Meanwhile, Margery was frantically getting into her sailor outfit and we both went on and did a comedy-themed tap dance dressed as sailors.

As soon as that was over, the other two girls came on in their finale costumes, which were red and white taffeta outfits, while we hurriedly changed and joined up for the big tapping finale.

As the finale ended, we were always cheered on for an encore. We could hardly breathe and we were puffing out the words to explain what the encore would be: "For an encore, we will now do an impersonation of a train leaving the station, going full speed, and then slowly coming to a halt at the next station."

Without any musical accompaniments, we did the train impersonation starting slowly, gathering speed, building to a rapid crescendo, until finally slowing down again and coming to "a stop at a station."

It was all with our feet, all in tap. It was demanding; but it was a fantastic routine.

The applause confirmed it!

We would do six evening shows and two matinees each week.

On Monday mornings we'd have a rehearsal; band call as it was referred to. We went through all the music and every part of the program with the orchestra. Then lighting and props had to be decided on. It was trial and error to find out what worked best.

* * *

Eventually, we took "The Four Petite Ascots" show on the road, with bookings in several different towns.

We had quite a few bookings, which was really good considering that was during The Depression of the 1930s. In England, that era of huge unemployment, strikes, and other types of economic discord was not thought of as The Great Depression—as the era was in the United States—but it was called only The Depression. Still, it was hard times for many people.

While we rehearsed, we were supposed to keep up our schooling. So we would go to the local school each morning, wherever we happened to be, and receive some instruction. We did some lessons in the afternoons as well, if we didn't have a matinee that day.

Of course, we never really learned anything because they would just stick us in a classroom. I had no favorite subject. In fact, I was hopeless at every subject—forget it. School was rote.

I learned later that some pretty famous people had also found school uninspiring and boring, such as the great physicist Albert Einstein. Needless to say, I am no Albert Einstein, by anyone's imagining. But knowing about his school troubles can be comforting to persons whose minds are also on other things besides mechanically repeating multiplication tables. My mind was on my desire to take my place in the theater spotlight.

Being in what we called "variety shows," there would be a couple of headliners and people who always had a top spot. We traveled each week to a different town. In those days every town had a theater, and the bigger the town, the bigger the theater.

We attended different types of schools, and had people who looked after us when we toured. Knowing we were in show business, the people we met treated us very well. In fact, they often treated us like celebrities.

Margery's older sister, who kind of chaperoned us around, would travel with us. The manager always reserved a certain number of train carriages for us, and some for the props.

I never missed a train call to travel on to the next city where we were booked to perform; I never got tired. I loved the whole thing. It was a super life, and we were a terrific act, with marvelous variety.

Eventually, my mother met another dancing teacher, Madame Bettina. She was in charge of a group of a dozen children called "The Mayfair Babes." Madame Bettina made us an offer we jumped at.

"If Pauline would leave 'The Four Petite Ascots,' she could do a complete solo with 'The Mayfair Babes,' " she said.

That, of course, appealed to my mother very much. So she went to talk to Dougie about this, knowing he wouldn't be happy. He showed her the contract we had with him. It said that I was supposed to stay in the act.

"Here. I have the contract," Dougie stated, waving it in the air.

My mother grabbed the contract out of his hand and tore it up.

"Well now she is no longer under contract," she informed him.

Then she signed a new contact on my behalf with "The Mayfair Babes."

I danced with the children in various routines. Soon, I had my very own solo.

I came onstage, sang one chorus of "Okay Toots," and did three choruses of hectic tap dancing.

The first town on our tour was Canterbury. Everywhere we appeared we always looked for a write-up in the local newspapers. In the very first week that I started working with the show, after our opening night, I went to buy the local newspaper to see if I'd get a write-up.

The reporter made some very complimentary remarks about the children. Then he wrote:

"Little Miss Pink ... (I knew he meant me because I was wearing a little pink dress) brings down the house with her hurricane tap dancing to 'Okay Toots.' "

I bought about five newspapers that day and sent one to all the relatives.

* * *

Because England is a monarchy, as well as having a parliamentary system of government, top performing artists are sometimes invited to participate in charity shows, and appear before whoever happens to be royalty at that time.

Many big name stars have appeared in the Royal Command Performances over the years, including Noel Coward, Ronald Reagan, Elizabeth Taylor, Vivien Leigh, and later, The Beatles, in 1963. By that time, however, the annual event was called Royal Variety Performance. King George V started the long-standing tradition, in 1912.

There is no pay for the entertainers who just offer their

services. All the money from the ticket sales goes to charities, primarily to the Entertainment Artists Benevolent Fund. Always, a member of the royal family is expected to attend.

We knew it was a great honor to appear in a Royal Command Performance, and one day Madame Bettina received a letter indicating that "The Mayfair Babes" had received such an honor. We were to appear before the Prince of Wales at the Alhambra Theatre, a grand, iconic venue in the West End of London.

At that time, Prince Edward, the son of King George V and Queen Mary, held the title, Prince of Wales.

Edward was handsome and popular, and his image appeared not only in many newspapers and magazines, but also on the front of a wide range of packaged commodities, including tins of mustard, tins of tea leaves, and boxes of chocolates produced under various brand names.

Apparently the tradition of placing the images of the royals on packaging increased sales.

Madame Bettina, whose name was really Betty, was asked if we would like to participate in the Royal Command Performance with two numbers: a kicking routine and a tap dance. We were to dress in pink and white outfits for the kicking routine, and then make a quick change into our red, white and blue costumes with white satin pants and pert little hats, and perform a military-style tap dance. Our blue satin tops were decorated with strips of gold braids across the front.

The Alhambra Theatre was much larger than any other theater I had performed in before. On the day of the performance, the theater was packed. As we prepared to go onstage, Madame Bettina hovered around, making sure everyone was ready and every costume was spotless. We were all very excited.

As we danced, a full orchestra accompanied us, and thankfully it went off without a hitch.

For the second dance, we mimicked soldiers going on parade. I was the "sergeant" leading the march, so my uniform was a little bit fancier than the others, with more gold braids across the chest and epaulets on the shoulders.

Just before we started to dance, part of the act required that one girl in the line put her foot forward a moment to soon. I had to point at her and say, "Wait for it, wait for it."

That got a big laugh.

Then the dance started and we paraded our tapping talents to the delight of the audience.

"The Mayfair Babes" received one of its biggest rounds of applause ever for that performance.

After the show, the Prince of Wales came backstage to meet us. He congratulated all the performers. We were still dressed in our military costumes. He came up to us and said how very much he enjoyed our dancing.

At that moment, I thought, "My cup runneth over."

CHAPTER 4

Me and the BBC

While we were traveling, I still wanted to keep reading my favorite newspaper comic strip. It featured a little bear named Rupert, who got into all kinds of adventures. He tangled with magicians, quirky professors, meteorologists who messed with the weather, and talking fish, birds and pixies. But he always managed to find his way back home by the end of each story, just in time for supper.

He was always depicted wearing a red sweater, yellow trousers and a checkered yellow scarf. *The Daily Express* Christmas annuals, featuring the adventures of Rupert Bear, were prized by millions of children in Britain, and I read my share.

When I was away, my mother would have to cut out the cartoon from the newspaper everyday and send it on to me to keep up with Rupert's daring deeds.

The little bear was created by illustrator and storyteller, Mary Tourtel, for publication in *The Daily Express* in the early part of the 20th century. For many years after that, Alfred Bestall created the enchanting pictures and stories.

The newspaper, featuring Rupert Bear's adventures, still circulates nationwide and Rupert seemed as popular as ever, last time I checked.

At a very early age, when my father was in town, he would teach me to read. He would bring home beautiful, secondhand children's books. Once I had read them they would disappear. He would exchange them for some others. He brought home some really wonderful books for me to read, and I wish I could have kept them.

During summer seasons each year, we were not touring. Instead, "The Mayfair Babes" show was asked to entertain passengers on the pleasure boat steamers taking day-trips from London to the seaside town of Margate.

The director of the steamboat company would hire us to perform four times a week. "The Mayfair Babes" were to entertain the passengers on the ship, both on the outbound ride to Margate, and also for the return trip in the evening.

Most of the passengers were families with children who were on holiday and wanted an inexpensive day-trip to the seaside town. The pleasure boat directors thought it would be nice to have children provide the entertainment; lunch was included.

We left early in the morning and did one show on board going out; the trip took about two hours.

When we arrived at Margate, we could do as we wished

for two or three hours, before sailing back in the evening. We were allowed to enjoy ourselves on the sands eating ice cream and playing games. We didn't go into the town; we stayed on the beach with a lady in charge of keeping an eye on us all. She would count heads to make sure we all got back on the boat again.

On the return journey, we did two shows on board—albeit sometimes with a few less performers.

The reduction in the number of tap dancers was due to eating too much ice cream or too many sweets, while playing on the beach, and then getting seasick while sailing home on the boat that rolled from side to side. But there were always enough of us left to perform during the return trip to London.

Going out to Margate, there were twelve young dancers. Coming back, there were usually only ten who could actually perform. But those of us who didn't overindulge, danced all the way back to London.

I was the soloist on these tours, doing my "Okay Toots" number.

But one day, I ate too many cherries in Margate. On the homeward voyage I regretted it, because I was throwing up all over the place. So, then there were nine, because three of us were hung over the railings of the steamer being sick. Those trips were always eventful.

"The Mayfair Babes" were contracted to perform on the boat for two summers, always during the month of August. It was one of my most enjoyable experiences as a member of that group.

Although The Depression was dragging down much of the

economy at this time, it really didn't bother us. At the time, I didn't even know there was a depression. My mother was still working at Dayl's Theater, in Leicester Square, where she was the assistant manager; I was dancing and filming, getting a guinea a day here and there.

My father was supporting himself because he was one of the last of the big spenders—spending mostly on himself.

We were managing, but still, people wondered how we could afford dance lessons.

"Pauline pays for her own dancing lessons," my mother would often say proudly. "She pays for it all herself with her own money."

She was also very proud of naming me "Pauline." I was named after the English silent movie actress, Pauline Frederick, my mother's favorite actress. Frederick, who later moved to America to make "talkies," also had only one daughter. She died in California in 1938.

Frankly, I didn't really like the name Pauline very much, but you take what you get.

After a few tours with "The Mayfair Babes," there were no booking dates for a while.

My next endeavor was to be in a radio spot. My agent arranged for it and said I should go to the BBC studio to appear on a radio variety show called *Tea Time Mixture*. I was to play a naughty child.

The show was so successful, that after a few weeks of being broadcasted every day at 5 p.m. all over Britain, we were told we would be heard soon in the United States. Only the name of the show would be changed.

However, there was a catch. Because of the time difference, we had to come to the studio at 4 a.m. so the BBC could broadcast the show live to the United States.

When it was 4 a.m. in England it would be 11 p.m. in New York, and 10 p.m. in Chicago. My mother came with me, of course, because it was the middle of the night. I was excited—but tired. I was the only child that was performing, and I had to stand on a soapbox to reach the microphone.

When we broadcasted *Tea Time Mixture* during the daytime, my mother stayed at home so she could hear me on the radio. She was my biggest fan. I would travel on my own by tube to the studio for the daytime broadcasts. I was only nine or ten years old, but I was used to going places on my own, if she couldn't take me. I would just hop on a bus, or the tube, and go; I was very independent.

One day in 1935, I got another message from my agent who said that a Major Green, British Army retired, was looking for a British girl who had been in British films, and who could be in one of Hughie Green's radio shows. Hughie Green was the major's son and the major promoted his radio and film work.

Hughie Green and His Gang was a popular radio show featuring teenagers singing a variety of songs.

"Would you like to go and audition for him?" the agent inquired.

He didn't have to ask me twice. So I went to see this Major Green. He was middle-aged, very business-like and kind of fierce-looking.

"You've heard of my son, Hughie, in *Hughie Green and his*

Gang on the wireless," the major stated briskly, rather than asked.

"He's just made his first movie, *Midshipman Easy*. I want someone to interview him on the wireless, asking him about this film. But it must be someone who has already been in movies," he growled.

My mother had already told him what I had done in films; he approved of me.

"I think you will work very well with him," the major declared, and gave me a script to memorize.

When I arrived at the BBC studio, I met Hughie and this gang of children that he worked with. He was quite tall for his age, about 14 or 15 years old at that time—I assumed. So, once again I had to stand on a soapbox to reach the microphone.

First Hughie interviewed me and asked me all about myself.

Then I said, "Oh, Hughie, I believe you've made a film."

And we went into a dialogue about *Midshipman Easy* and how he was starring in it.

I was just lucky to get that radio part. I got paid five guineas for doing it.

I never saw Hughie personally again. I did see the movie; it was very good.

He did a lot of radio shows and production work as he grew up. But it seemed that his father ruled him with a rod of iron.

I wouldn't have wanted to be in Hughie Green's "gang." I don't think I could have worked for the major.

Meanwhile, my mother was filming with the cast of *The Man Who Knew Too Much*. The 1934 thriller was later made with Jimmy Stewart and Doris Day. But in the earlier version, my mother played one of the women sitting in the little church, where the parents of a kidnapped boy search for their son. A terror group was holding the child prisoner.

Films always intrigued me, and I was chosen in 1935 to appear in a child's role in Alfred Hitchcock's film, *Sabotage*. The film was based on the novel by Joseph Conrad called, *The Secret Agent*.

The storyline was that a Scotland Yard detective was on the trail of a gang of saboteurs. They were terrorists funded by a foreign government, attempting to set off a bomb in London.

In the film, I appear in the scene with a group of children who discover what looks like a dead body. We find out it was Sylvia Sidney, who had fainted. I'm the one in the white beret.

One night, during a filming session in London, I gave my mother a real scare. She was not needed for filming at the studio the day it happened. So she gave a few shillings to a friend of hers, who was filming, to take care of me and to make sure that I got home safely.

The friend met me at the tube station and made sure I got to the studio.

"Go and get your makeup on and your costume," she said, when we arrived. She went off to do her studio work, and I was on my own.

At five o'clock, when we were finishing up and getting

ready to be paid, the director asked if everybody would like to work overtime. Of course everybody did, because we always received time-and-a-half pay for overtime work.

The producer wanted the children to stay with the rest of the actors, and it got to be around 10 p.m. before he was ready to call it quits. My mother's friend was continuing to keep an eye on me.

By the time we took our makeup off and lined up for our pay, it was close to 11 p.m. Unfortunately, the buses had stopped running to the tube stations, so we were all worried about how we were going to get back home.

"We will hire some cars to take you to your homes," the assistant director told us.

Because we didn't have a telephone at home then, the lady looking after me couldn't let my mother know why I was so late.

My mother was working at Daly's Theater that night, and got in at about 9 p.m. She asked my cousin, Mary, who was staying with us at the time, if I was already asleep in bed.

"Oh no, Pauline hasn't come home yet," Mary said.

My mother couldn't believe it and went frantic right away. "Where is she?" she demanded.

Of course, Mary didn't know.

My mother rushed down to the tube station and watched the last train come in … No Pauline!

By that time she was panicking and finally went to the local police station and said that I was missing. It was gone 11 p.m. I don't know what reason she gave, as to why I should be out that late at night.

"She is definitely missing," she told the police, in no uncertain terms.

A call went out to all the police stations. Officers and constables were told to be on the alert and to look for me.

Meanwhile, the black limousine that I was in drew up in front of our block of flats. I waltzed into the building and went upstairs. When I knocked on our door and my cousin opened it, she threw her arms around me.

"My God, you've got half the police in London looking for you," she said. "Quick, get into bed!"

About half an hour later, my mother, who by now was in tears, came up to the flat to see if there was any word of me.

My cousin said, "She's fine. She's in bed."

My mother immediately came into the bedroom and said, "That's it. No more filming. I can't go through this again."

Then, after a moment of silence: "What happened?" she demanded.

I explained to her about the overtime work that night, and how nice it was to come home in a limousine.

"Everybody was happy to work overtime because we got paid extra for that," I said.

I was quite happy about the whole thing, particularly when I presented her with my pay, including overtime. But she wasn't mollified; she had made up her mind. I was never to go down to the studios again.

Then she went back to the police station to inform them that I was now at home safe and sound. What story she gave them then I can't imagine.

Soon after that episode, we had a telephone installed. About three weeks later, we got a call for me to go down to the studios. So off I went.

Now that we had a phone we could communicate more successfully. Most other film extras didn't have telephones. They had to rely on a messaging system to summon them to an audition if they weren't at the film guildhall.

Everyday, most of them would sit in the guild facility and someone from the production would select the people they wanted for a film project. The extras would be sitting there, practically all day and everyday, waiting for work. They could get a cup of tea cheaply, or a roll to eat.

They had a very poor lifestyle. Most of them lived in one room with a gas ring and shared a toilet. They were dependent on that guinea for the work, if they were called to film.

The studio might need a certain type of person, or several extras. Sometimes they would want two or three children. The lucky ones would be told that they would be working the next day, and that they should go down to the studio.

If the film needed a costume, they would be told what to wear. The film might require street clothes, evening dress or uniforms.

There was a resale shop nearby where wealthy stars, who became tired of their clothes or who wanted new clothes, would donate their old things to the shop. The extras would go there once a week and pick out decent clothing very cheaply, even evening dress, which made great costumes.

Acting has never failed to delight me. But for making films, there's no place like Hollywood.

One day, not long after my 13th birthday, my mother came into my room with a bunch of brochures.

"I've decided that we are going to go to America," she announced.

CHAPTER 5

California, Here I Come!

My mother was excited.

"I would like to see Hollywood, and if we don't work or do anything out there, we will consider it a very interesting trip. I would like to go on the quota system, and then we can stay in the country," she said.

I didn't have any say about this plan. I thought to myself that it could be an interesting adventure. I was never afraid to try something new.

We had to get on the quota list and wait for U.S. immigration to call us, because there are only so many people allowed into the United States each year, we learned.

"I've managed to get us passage on the *Queen Mary*," my mother told me, after our visas and other paperwork required for traveling came through.

"That will be the third voyage the *Queen Mary* has ever

made to the United States. We are to go to New York first, then go on to California," she explained.

My mother never mentioned anything to my father about going. He was always gone so much anyway. My mother sublet our apartment to Madame Bettina, and sold all the furniture to help fund our trip. There was so much money involved in this adventure. We knew that, basically, we didn't have a home to come back to.

Finally we were ready, and we sailed out of Southampton on a clear day in 1936.

Instead of enjoying the voyage on the *Queen Mary*, the weather became rough, and we were so seasick that we stayed in our bunks. Neither of us slept. All we could keep down was dry crackers and water.

Once we arrived in America, we stayed three days in New York with the sister of a woman that my mother worked with in London. Because you had to have someone to sponsor you into the country—a relative—this woman made out she was my mother's cousin.

We met her for the first time when we arrived in New York, and stayed with her in Flushing, Long Island, for about three or four days, to recuperate from our sea sickness. We did a little sightseeing around New York, which consisted mostly of shopping.

Then we took a Greyhound bus from New York to California, and of course, Hollywood. We saw something of the country going out there. It took a good week.

We arrived in Los Angeles and my mother naturally thought all the studios were around Hollywood so that's where we should live. She managed to rent a small apartment in Hollywood. As it so happened, only one studio was in Hollywood. All the rest were way outside in Burbank and different places.

However, she did find an agent for me without much trouble. He said he would look into things and see if they needed a little English girl to say a few lines for whatever was going on at the time.

In the meantime, I auditioned at the radio station KFAC. The station was putting on the life of David Windsor, the Prince of Wales, from his childhood on. They wanted a little English girl to play Princess Mary. So I auditioned, and with my strong British accent, I got the part.

It was a series. It went on once a week for about four weeks. Ironically, the Prince of Wales was played by a little Japanese girl, with a very strong, boyish English accent.

I couldn't believe it. This little Japanese girl comes on and she was playing the Prince of Wales with the deep voice and a British accent. It was amazing, and a little startling.

From then on, I did some radio work whenever they needed a child with a British accent.

I finally found that I had to go back to school, because the "school-leaving age" was close to 18 in California; in England it was 14 years of age.

So I went to Brancroft Junior High School. It was totally different from an English school. I was constantly getting lost trying to find different classrooms. But nobody was expecting very much of me. Because I was English, it was believed that I had already had plenty of academics under my belt.

I told them I had studied different subjects at the English schools I had attended. All they seemed concerned with was learning about the Indians, which I knew nothing about. In Hollywood, classrooms were like playgrounds, with girls jumping up and down, talking back to the teacher. To me it was just chaos.

However, I did make at least one friend. There was a chubby, little dark-haired girl, about my age who sat next to me in sewing class. She was about as dumb as I was when it came to using the sewing machine, so we spent most of our time giggling and making fun of people.

But this little girl, not even 5 feet tall, had a terrific voice and she would entertain us on Fridays in the gym, belting out some songs.

Although she was little, she was soon to become very big in the entertainment world. By the way, she would become known as Judy Garland.

She wasn't called Judy Garland when she was introduced to us. She was known by her real name, Frances (Judy) Gumm.

One Friday, after she had performed for us, the principal (head master) of the school came on the stage and announced, "We have to say goodbye to little Judy now. She has signed a contract with Metro-Goldwyn-Mayer and she will be going to the studio school from now on," the principal said.

She was soon to become a world-renowned starlet most recognized as Dorothy Gale, in *The Wizard of Oz*. That famous film was released in 1939.

Judy was like me. She was all for her career; and she had a mother who would push, push, push.

My mother was a wonderful woman actually. Her life was more or less dedicated to me. She had a beautiful voice. I think if she had had the money to train her voice she would have become quite a well-known singer.

She had many fine qualities, however, she couldn't cook at all, except during the war when food was rationed. All of a sudden, she became quite a good cook because she couldn't afford to spoil anything.

She was a very good mother to me in every way. I'm glad she pushed me because I thought I wasn't that bright, and I probably couldn't have done anything else for a living. At least, that's what I believed at the time.

We were staying in a bungalow on Las Palmas Avenue, in Hollywood, which was rented to us by a very old man. He had two or three other bungalows on his land that he was renting out.

He also had an old friend who was a miner, who seemed to spend his time discovering oil wells. He seemed to have quite a few wealthy people who were investing in his oil projects.

One evening, our landlord introduced my mother to his old friend. She explained why we were in California, and that she wanted me to see as much as possible, while we were there.

The elderly man said he had many connections. "I'm a good friend of Sid Grauman, who is a co-owner the Grauman's Chinese Theatre, and a master showman. He is one of my investors. Maybe I could take Pauline out to dinner one night, at Sid's favorite restaurant. We might meet him there and I could introduce Pauline to him," he suggested.

My mother agreed to let me go. I dressed up in my prettiest party dress and off we went.

We had a very nice dinner at the Cocoanut Grove, in the Ambassador Hotel, in Los Angeles.

I was fascinated with all the artificial palm trees and the ceiling that was inlaid with lights that looked like sparkling stars. Most of all, I welcomed the chance to see film stars who came there to dine. I learned it was one of the stars' favorite places for dining and dancing. So I kept busy, looking to see what famous faces I could spot.

Unfortunately, when our delightful dinner ended I was in for a shock. My friend found out that he had forgotten his wallet; we couldn't pay for the meal!

At that point, I was sure I would soon get to see what the kitchen looked like—we'd be washing dishes to pay for our high-class dinner!

I was so embarrassed, and getting into a panic, I was ready to crawl under the table.

My friend called the headwaiter and tried to explain to him that he didn't have any money with him, when he suddenly spotted Sid Grauman. My friend went over and explained our predicament.

"That's perfectly all right. I'll pick up the check," the generous Grauman said.

I breathed a big sigh of relief and vowed never to go out and have dinner with this gentleman again.

While that friendship didn't last, the fabulously adorned

Chinese Theatre did. It is an historic landmark and a well-known fixture of Hollywood architecture. Many red carpet and premiere events are still held there today.

* * *

While in California, I auditioned at MGM studios for a speaking role in the film *Night Must Fall*, the 1937 thriller with Robert Montgomery, Rosalind Russell and Dame May Whitty.

The audition was held at one of the sound studios. I stood in a line with a large number of other teenagers. We were trying out for the part of an English-speaking girl. I was 14 years old.

One of the assistant directors came in and surveyed us. "As I'm going down the line, I want you each to say, with a Cockney accent, 'Give me your autograph,' " he instructed.

One by one, all the kids were saying the line with American accents.

When he came to me, I said the line with the boldness of a native Londoner, "Giv'me your au' agraph" (Cockney's don't sound their T's).

Pointing at me, the assistant director said, "I'll take that one."

That's how I came to appear in *Night Must Fall*.

We went up to Lake Tahoe to film, with Robert Montgomery playing the leading man's role, which was a creepy young man working as a companion for an old lady. Her young niece suspected the companion of murder.

I remember wearing a plaid dress, and a wide-brimmed

straw hat that someone found for me in one of the cabins at the lake. The setting was supposed to be in front of an English cottage.

The scenery for the location shots was stunningly rough, but beautiful. Buses took us up to the lake for a day of filming, and brought us back at night. The rest of the movie was filmed in the studio.

It was during the California rainy season when we finished filming *Night Must Fall.* But I realized they had forgotten to pay me the extra dollars, which were due to me because I had a speaking part.

So my agent said that I should go back to the studio and they would give me the extra money. So I went back to seek out the studio office. It was pouring with rain, but I found shelter in front of one of the sound stages.

Suddenly, a door to the sound stage opened and a lady in full Edwardian costume came out, with another lady holding an umbrella over her.

They were getting ready to cross the road and I thought I should ask them directions:

"Can you tell me where I go to get this extra pay? Is there an office nearby?" I inquired.

"Oh yes, I believe there's an office just across the street. If you like, you can share our umbrella," one of the women said. She was well-spoken and had a slight accent.

"Oh, thank you very much," I replied, and we all ventured across the street through the downpour.

In the office, one of the men, who had been standing outside when we crossed the road, surprised me with a question.

"Do you know who you shared the umbrella with?"

"No."

"That was Garbo," he said.

Greta Garbo was filming at the same studio at that time. She had so much makeup on and was in full period costume that it didn't dawn on me who she was.

When she offered to share her umbrella with me, I heard her accent, but I didn't place her. I always thought she was taller than she was in real life. But that can be true of so many larger-than-life film stars.

A few years earlier, Garbo had played a leading lady in a film about a double agent spying for Germany and/or France during World War I. The movie was *Mata Hari*, filmed in 1931. The true story was about a Dutch woman who chose the name Mata Hari when she became an exotic dancer, and—it is believed—a spy. She was suspected of being a double agent for either the French or the Germans, or both during WWI.

Mata Hari performed her dances throughout Europe, until she met a rather sudden end. The French executed her in 1917, by firing squad for spying.

The name Mata Hari soon became synonymous with intrigue, espionage, female double agents, and in fact was a household word in England and probably across Europe as well.

I can't think of a better actress to play the female spy than the sultry Greta Garbo. She was perfect for that part.

I could hardly believe that I had shared an umbrella with one of Hollywood's greatest leading ladies of the time. I hoped some of her talent had rubbed off on me.

That chance encounter was one for my memory book.

In Hollywood you never knew what to expect, or whom you might run into from one minute to the next, rain or shine, under storm clouds, or somewhere beyond a rainbow.

CHAPTER 6

Tap, Don't Jump

When I worked at a studio in California, I would go to the studio school each day. Every studio had to have a classroom and a teacher. We were supposed to have a certain number of hours a day of instruction. But we never abided by the rule, because as soon as we would get settled down, there would suddenly be a call to go on the set and that would be it.

They never kept to the rules of how many hours you were supposed to have for academic instruction.

Dancing remained my main focus. At the first opportunity, I auditioned in Hollywood before yet another dance teacher.

"Where did you learn to tap like that?" he asked.

"In England," I said confidently.

"That's old fashioned; we don't tap like that. You're jumping up and down tapping," he said.

"You need to watch Eleanor Powell. Her feet hardly leave the ground—she's just doing the beats," he said.

Powell used what has been called "machine-gun" footwork. She appeared in films with the likes of Fred Astaire. They danced together to Cole Porter's "Begin the Beguine."

So I had a lot to aspire to if I was to be like Eleanor Powell. I had to learn a whole new system of tap dancing.

To make sure I did it correctly, by keeping my feet on the ground, the teacher would hold a board over my head. If my head hit the board I wasn't doing it right.

I couldn't jump up and down anymore. I had to stay on the ground. It took a lot to learn that technique. But it stood me in good stead, because when I came back to England, hardly anybody was doing the American tap. It was a big help, in my career path.

I loved California, because when I was there, smog was unheard of. Not many cars were on the roads then, and that meant no smog at all.

You could set the date by when the rainy season was going to start and going to end.

Most of the time the weather was glorious. That was good because I used bus connections and transfer tickets to get to the various studios. As I stood waiting at bus stops, I was bathed in the warm California sunshine almost everyday.

At first though, we didn't understand about bus transfers. We had never heard of them in England at that time. We'd be paying our bus fares over and over again, as we went from one bus to another, instead of buying transfer tickets.

There were times in our new country when money was short. So my mother did some babysitting.

The thing about moving to a whole "new world" is that you never know what you'll find there until you actually arrive. It is a gutsy thing to move to another land on the other side of the world far from friends, family and all that's familiar.

But my mother was a gutsy lady. I like to think I inherited her élan.

* * *

When we had been in California for two years, we started hearing rumors of war. Things in Europe were getting a bit dicey.

My aunts wrote to my mother and said maybe you should come back to your own country. "You've been out there for two years," they frequently reminded us in their letters.

They thought it would be safer to be back in England!

During that time, Nazi Germany, under Adolf Hitler had broken the Treaty of Versailles by marching into the Rhineland, which was declared a demilitarized zone after Germany's defeat in World War I.

We hadn't really noticed what was going on in other countries. We were enjoying sunny California so much.

The dangerous situation in Europe was overshadowed in England by the abdication of Edward VIII, who left the English throne and his people, after only a few months, so he could marry a divorced American woman named Wallace Simpson.

That created a constitutional crisis, because kings of England were not supposed to marry divorced women.

But he was admired by many young women for giving up so much for the woman he loved. Edward was almost as much of a heartthrob in some quarters as Rudolf Valentino, although the man who would not be king was also not an actor.

He certainly wasn't acting when he went on the radio in Britain and declared his love for Mrs. Simpson. Many people loved him for his honesty. He announced his abdication from the throne a few days before Christmas, 1936.

But living safely in California, we were a long way away from kings and dictators.

We were oblivious to the encroaching Nazi armies, and the death camps that were being built to burn people alive in Germany and Poland. We were oblivious also to the building up of the Japanese military, and to British Prime Minister Neville Chamberlain's apparent belief that being nice to Hitler was the way to secure peace.

But our relatives in England saw the danger coming and pressed for our return home.

Also, my father, having found out that we had disappeared to America, was making noises about taking his child out of the country without his permission. Not that he really cared, but he just wanted to make a show of something.

So, finally we decided to go back. However, we dreaded the voyage after being seasick so much on the trip over to the U.S.A.

"We will not go on the *Queen Mary* again," my mother

announced, "because they haven't yet put stabilizers on that ship."

Not wanting to experience a horribly rough crossing a second time, we booked on a different ocean liner. A month before we were to set sail, the ship we were booked on burned down, while in New York Harbor.

Shortly afterward, we got a notice saying: "You are very lucky you've been transferred to the *Queen Mary*."

So we took another Greyhound bus back to New York and spent a couple of nights in a hotel before boarding the *Queen Mary* once again.

We got to our births and were seasick all the way back across the Atlantic. The steward brought us lots of dry crackers and water. That was all we could stomach until we reached dry land again.

* * *

I was 15 in 1938, when we arrived back in England. Madame Bettina, my former dance teacher, was still living in our old apartment and we could not turn her out. We managed to get a room at a boarding house for a few weeks until we finally found a flat.

Our flat was in Covent Garden next to some solicitors' offices. It was the only available flat in Broad Court. On the corner was a police station; across the road was the famous Covent Garden Opera House.

My mother always wanted to be in the center of London. She didn't want to be outside the vibrant capital city with its important entertainment sector.

But she knew that she would have to go back to work to help support us. We rejoined the Film Artists Association. I started filming and advertising again; and she got a job managing a bar at a racetrack.

It was a difficult time. We hadn't heard from my father at all, and we had no idea where he was.

There could be no doubt about the serious international situation.

Early the following year, one of the first signs of real trouble was an article in the newspaper asking all available people to go to the London parks and start digging trenches. The idea was that if someone was caught out during an air raid, if they were near a park, they could dive into a trench and possibly save their life—possibly.

Mainly, it was women who went to dig the trenches because the men were already being called up for military duty.

All the sod that came out of the trenches was piled into sandbags. Those sandbags were used to put up against the buildings throughout the city. They were piled up one on top of the other because if a bomb fell nearby, the chances were that the sandbagged building would withstand the blast.

One morning, to my amazement as I was walking down Piccadilly, I happened to look up in the sky and was startled by what I saw. Hundreds of silver balloons were wafting around way up high. Everywhere I looked there were balloons.

They were all over the sky tethered to earth by long wires. I asked a soldier working nearby what they were doing.

"Those are there because if the Germans come and

fly over London, they may get tangled in the wires of the balloons, and that will bring the planes down," he said.

I thought to myself, "Oh dear, this is beginning to sound very ominous. I hope the balloons' wires can help keep us safe."

Clearly, Chamberlain's peace pact with Hitler had given us about six months to get prepared for another large scale war, a world war as it turned out. Perhaps that had been Chamberlain's plan all along. He may have wanted to buy us some time to get ready for the worst-case scenario.

Two weeks later, we received a postcard in the mail stating that we should go to the local school in the evening, and be measured for our gas masks. That's when my mother came to the conclusion that war was inevitable.

The reason for the imperative that we all have gas masks was that during World War I, poison gas had been used against our troops. No one knew if gas would be used against the civilian population in future conflicts or not, but it was a big concern.

So we went to our nearest school, and in the basement were men with big boxes full of black gas masks. Hundreds of people were lining up.

"Try these on, Luv. One at a time now, there you are. How's that?" the men inquired.

The gas mask distributors were trying to sound matter-of-fact and trying to reassure us that it was quite natural to wear these ugly things on our faces. As we were being fitted, it seemed like we were supposed to think we were trying on new hats.

We had to select a mask that was a very close fit, so no gas could seep in.

They were nasty, smelly things with long snouts. They made us all look like anteaters. We were told if war was declared we were to carry them with us all the time. We were instructed never to leave our homes without our gas masks.

Of course, you couldn't put a gas mask on a baby, so they had special cylinders that looked like little beds inside the suitcase-sized containers. The cylinders had Plexiglas-type tops that shut tight. If there was a gas raid, there was a knob on top you would turn to filter out the gas. Don't ask me how the babies could breath in those things!

If an air raid happened, the babies were to be quickly placed in the contraptions, in case poison gas was dropped. Parents were given instructions on the way to turn the knobs so that any gas that seeped in would be filtered out of the little cylinders.

As it turned out, the Germans did not use gas warfare against us in the Second World War, because they knew if they did we would retaliate in kind. They didn't want to take a chance on that.

* * *

That winter, I was lucky enough to get booked in a Christmas Pantomime, *Dick Whittington* at the Palace Theater, in Hammersmith. I was part of the chorus.

It was lucky partly because I faked my age and told them I was 17. The show, a cheerful production, was to run for approximately three weeks.

One evening after the curtain came down, my father showed up at the stage door. I don't know how he knew I was working in the show, because by that time I had changed my surname to Fraser.

I changed my surname because everybody seemed to spell my real last name, Mabbett, incorrectly. Fraser was simpler to print on the billboards and programs for the shows. While my name was not in the biggest print, it was on the main announcements for many of the shows in which I performed.

My father invited me out to supper, and we had quite a long chat. I told him about all the wonders I had seen in California.

He told me he had an apartment somewhere in London. But, he thought he would like to move back in with us again, which he did.

He was between shows at the time.

I was about to make my debut as a glamorous Windmill girl.

And Britain was on the verge of the fight of its life.

CHAPTER 7

In the Windmill's Legendary Spotlight

The pantomime, *Dick Whittington*, had so many stars in it that instead of running for a month, and finishing after Christmas was over as most pantomimes do, it continued on for four months into the spring of 1939, ending with two weeks in Oxford.

The pay was three pounds a week, which was very good in those days.

By that time we were living in a flat on Charing Cross Road, near the Windmill Theatre, which was in Piccadilly on Great Windmill Street. In the early 20th Century, the site, then a small playhouse, was used to film some of the first silent movies.

One day in the spring, I heard that the theater needed short girls as dancers. So faking my age again, I auditioned.

The stage was quite small at the Windmill, and all the

girls of the chorus line had to be short. I was only about 5 feet tall, and I was selected to be one of the eight-member dancing line.

It was to be a tough schedule, but I was ready and excited to be working in this avant-garde theater that took its cue from the *Moulin Rouge* and the *Folies Bergeres* in Paris, although I didn't know that at the time.

We dancers, of course, were all well dressed.

The set up was that we would work for three weeks, five shows a day. Then we would have a week off with pay to rest, and then two weeks rehearsal for a new show, while another company was performing.

I was excited because this was a big step up in my career, and a bonus was I could walk to the Windmill Theatre from our flat; the Soho area at that time was a respectable neighborhood.

After a strenuous rehearsal schedule, we were ready for the all-important dress rehearsal. As I prepared to go on, I noticed some beautiful-looking girls in the wings who didn't seem to be doing too much.

They weren't very short either. In fact, they were quite tall and stately looking.

They were just walking around, and I wondered what part of the show they were in. I thought to myself, "They couldn't be dancers because they never rehearsed with us."

Well, I was in for a shock.

I almost fainted as the girls stood on the stage and posed without moving, wearing nothing but a rose bud on each breast and a little jock strap.

Now there are rules, and the person to enforce those rules is called The Lord Chamberlain of London. In Will Shakespeare's time, the Lord of the Revels had the duty to check up on what was going on in the theaters. If a play was considered unacceptable, (such as allowing women to perform, which was forbidden at that time) he had the power to shut the place down. Of course, the rules have changed a lot in London in four hundred years or so.

The person running the Windmill had to answer to The Lord Chamberlain, and in our case that man was Vivian Van Damm, a highly intelligent Dutch Jewish man who ran the place like clockwork. He followed all the rules.

He knew that if a nude moved on the stage, it was considered obscene. But if there was no movement it was considered art, just like a nude statue in a museum.

The catch phrase was "If you move, it's rude."

Van Damm was hired as manager of the Windmill Theatre by Lady Laura Henderson, the owner of the theater. He became well-known for producing *The Revudeville* shows and a series of nude tableaux featuring "mermaids," "Native American Indians" and "Britannia" as the themes.

Van Damm was about 5 feet 6 inches in height. He wasn't a very tall man. He was striking more than handsome, with very dark penetrating eyes and dark wavy hair. We nicknamed him "V.D." I think he must have been aware of his nickname, but he never let on.

He was a master at lighting a show. There would be a lighting rehearsal and he would sit there and know exactly where the floodlights should go and what was the best way to manipulate the lighting.

He had a choreographer and a producer for the shows. However, he would take care of booking the comedian for most productions.

For each new production, he would have a ballerina from a London ballet company come in and be the soloist in our very short ballets. We had a little ballet performance in every show to give variety.

There were four or five of us who danced. We stuffed our toe shoes with clumps of cotton wool and onto the stage we went. We weren't really ballet dancers, but we had ballet training before we joined the company. Often, the premiere ballerinas came to us from the famous Sadler's Wells Ballet School and the Vic-Wells Ballet to star in that part of the show.

In contrast to Van Damm, Mrs. Henderson was a quiet person, and to my mind, she was not nearly as outgoing as she is portrayed in the 2005 film, *Mrs. Henderson Presents*.

I found her rather reserved. But she had nerve enough to put nudes in the show to try to draw bigger audiences.

It worked.

Lady Henderson was a sweet little old lady. However, she had the habit of walking into the dressing room without knocking. She always had a couple of fellows with her, usually titled men.

When these sudden appearances occurred, we would all dive for our dressing gowns.

This would often happen when we'd be in the middle of changing for our next act.

It got to the point where the showgirls would send down word: "Old Ma Henderson is in the theater. So get ready for her!"

The Henderson family was very wealthy. Mrs. Henderson was a widow when she bought the Windmill in 1931.

Van Damm's brilliance in running the theater was regularly confirmed, because we usually played to packed houses.

Later, when the German Luftwaffe roared overhead nightly and bombed London, some of the showgirls picked up on the V for victory symbol, made famous by Winston Churchill, and they used it when the show was underway during heavy air raids.

But when I was working at the Windmill, London was still enjoying a peaceful existence.

The Windmill was a very small theater; the backstage area was tiny. The stage itself was small and lit by colored lighting. The floor of the stage was covered with thick squares of glass that were lit by the various colored lights. The squares were sealed together with metal bars, which became very hot as the evening wore on.

If you happened to sit on the metal parts you soon discovered they were burning hot. If the choreography required you to sit down and you happened to sit on a metal bar you burnt your behind!

I had to sit during one of the shows with these lights shining underneath the stage floor and the metal bars heating up, and I can attest to the fact that they were hot!

The shows were regularly viewed and judged on whether the acts were appropriate or not. A lot of clergy came in whenever a new show opened. I suppose they were there to see if it was respectable or not. At least, we were told that they were there to make sure it was clean enough for the audience to enjoy.

Van Damm imposed tough rules on the performers. We were not allowed to go out with anybody who came around to the stage door. We were not allowed to mingle in any way with the audience. You had to go straight home after the last show.

If you decided to get married you would have to leave the Windmill. I suppose he feared the husbands might interfere in some way if their wives were performing there—V.D. didn't want any problems.

I know a couple of girls, who were quite prominent in the show, who were fired because they got married right after the war. They thought it important to get married before their men went back to their respective homelands.

They were among the approximately 70,000 war brides of WWII, who married military men from other nations— mostly from the United States. Of course, marriage put an end to their Windmill careers.

Life in the theater was busy that summer of 1939, with five shows a day keeping us in shape and giving us good appetites. It helped that a canteen was located at the top of the theater where you could go for a meal.

But we'd get so fuddled doing five shows a day for three weeks in a row. I was always asking someone if this is the third or the fourth show of the day; I would loose count.

But when it came to dancing, I never lost a beat.

CHAPTER 8

The Evacuation

That summer, while we were entertaining people from all walks of life, rumors of war were gathering steam. Soon the whispers of the possibility of war with Germany became as frequent as the sight of ravens circling the Tower of London.

In the streets of the city, beyond the walls of our small theater, there was tension in the air. But Londoners still went about their business as if nothing could ever really happen here.

I would return home in the early hours of the morning tired out from dancing, and flop into bed. That is except for one night in mid August, when my mother was waiting up for me with some news.

She read from a postcard that had arrived for us: "All men and women who can help, are asked to assist with the evacuation of the children from England's cities to safer locations in the countryside."

The government wasn't going to wait for the declaration of war to protect the citizenry.

The letter informed us they were going ahead with the evacuation right away, even though war had not yet been declared against us by Germany, or against Germany by us.

We knew, though, that if the "Jerries" as we called the German military, continued to invade other countries on the continent of Europe, England almost certainly would get into the fray, and try to put a stop to the aggression.

The postcard instructed us to be at King's Cross Station at 6 a.m. the next morning, and ride the train with the children. Then we were to make sure they met with suitable accommodations.

I had to get word to Van Damm that I wouldn't be able to be in the show for two or three days because I was helping with the evacuation. I knew he would not be happy.

Thank God he understood; he was a patriot.

So my mother and I were at the train station at six o'clock in the morning, ready to board. The station was packed with children, holding onto their belongings in little suitcases or traveling bags. They were all over the place; it was a madhouse. The station was full of crying mothers, crying children and screaming babies.

The evacuation at this time was voluntary, but it was advised that people evacuate immediately. We were instructed to bring our gas masks, if we had them. Luckily, we had already been fitted for ours.

Women volunteers were handing out cups of tea to pacify us. I had six children to watch over and my mother had 10.

A man came around and hung big labels on each of us with our names and addresses clearly marked. He also had to make sure everyone had a gas mask. The children all had their masks strung around their necks.

At the appointed hour, we all piled onto the evacuation trains. Mothers, who stayed back, waved tearful good-byes to their children. Only those mothers with very small infants or babies got on the trains with the rest of the evacuees.

We had no idea where we were going. Nobody would tell us our destinations.

My mother and I ended up in Bury St. Edmonds with dozens of children swarming around us as we got off the train. Coaches were waiting to take the reluctant travelers to a local school hall.

At the school, we sat on long benches and waited for residents to arrive and choose the children they would have stay with them. Slowly, the residents of the area gradually came in and selected whom they would take into their homes.

Some residents said they could take only one child. Others said that they could house two or three children. Some mothers, who were left behind in London, had instructed their offsprings to be sure to stay together. Nobody wanted siblings to be separated, but some were.

I noticed that the little girls who most resembled Shirley Temple were chosen first!

The mothers with babies were assigned homes. The children were taken at random.

It was compulsory to take a child if you had space and the government would pay for their room and board. Eventually, every child was selected to go to a new temporary home.

Some of the luckier children were taken to live in castles that had been taken over for such a purpose; and in some cases whole schools were billeted in castles. The children would eat, sleep, and have their lessons there.

I wondered though, if the moat had to be kept full and the drawbridge pulled up to keep some of them in line.

When everyone had left the school, my mother and I returned to the station, and just sat there hoping to get the next train back to London. But before the next train arrived, an Army officer came into the waiting room.

"What are you doing here?" he asked.

"Waiting for the next train back to London," we told him.

"Oh, you can't go back for at least two weeks. You have to go around to all the houses and see that everyone is settled in. We'll send a car for you every day to go visit every household," the officer said.

We didn't expect anything like that. I protested that I had a show to perform in; but it was to no avail.

So then I had to write another frantic letter to Vivian Van Damm saying I won't be back at the Windmill for two weeks.

I could just picture him with his neat wavy, dark brown hair, his firm chin, and his spiffy suit standing straight-backed, holding my letter and silently fuming about the loss of a dancer even though it was only for a couple of weeks.

We didn't know where we were going to stay in this town. It was so unfamiliar to us.

"There's a big estate not far from here. The manor house is owned by Americans," the Army officer said.

"They've gone back to the States; it's all boarded up. But the gamekeeper's cottage has an extra room. You can stay there with him and his wife, and we will pay for the room and board while you are there," he explained.

He drove us to the gates of the big estate. The cottage was just inside the property. It was a good-sized brick house. The gamekeeper and his wife were very nice and very kind to us.

The arrangement suited us fine. It was like a two-week vacation with glorious late summer weather.

Every day the Army officer would come in his car to collect my mother and she would go to visit all the various families where the evacuees were staying to see if there were any problems.

The children all seemed to be settling in very well. But some of the mothers with babies, after a week, began to worry and wonder what their husbands were doing in London without them being there.

As the days went by, the mothers became more and more nervous about being gone from their homes in the city. A few of them mentioned to my mother that they had decided to go back and take their chances.

There was nothing my mother could do. We couldn't very well tell them they should stay, because after all, we were going to go back ourselves.

Within a couple of weeks, when there were no signs of any bombing, many of the evacuees had drifted back to London. However, some of the more prudent parents waited to see what would happen, and let their children stay away from the cities.

Most of the children who were evacuated stayed for the duration of the war. They spent five years in these foster homes and they didn't return to the cities. It wasn't just London that had to evacuate the children, it was all the cities that the children had to be moved from, until the war was over.

But a lot of the children were already deciding they wanted to go back to their homes even after just a few weeks. Of course the decision was not up to them.

Five years in a foster home was a long time. Some of the children left London with real Cockney accents: "Cor' blimey, ain't aff …" was typically heard.

Some of them were billeted in very nice homes. When they went back to their own homes five years later, they weren't speaking in slang anymore. Words like "toffs" and "Cor' blimey, ain't aff" became "…isn't it a beautiful day, sir?"

The parents didn't know what to make of it because all those Cockney accents sort of disappeared over the five war years.

Our days in Bury St. Edmonds were filled with sunshine. I had the run of the extensive grounds, which were being kept up for the owners very nicely. We had some excellent meals there. I think the gamekeeper must have caught pheasant and rabbit in the area, and there was plenty of room to grow vegetables on the property. His wife was an excellent cook, so we ate our fill.

We were just enjoying ourselves immensely. Everything was so peaceful. The trees were so green and full of foliage, and I lazed under them reading and daydreaming, or sometimes I spent my days exploring the grounds of the estate.

As the late summer sunlight slowly spread patterns of gold on the deep green lawns, we could never have imagined the dark storm clouds that were to come.

On September 3, we were in church when war was declared.

Because Germany had continued its aggression and invaded Poland, Great Britain declared war on Germany. Neville Chamberlain, the prime minister, made the announcement over the wireless on that fateful Sunday morning.

* * *

We got back to London in a hurry. There were no air raids going on. In fact, things seemed quite normal.

I went back to the Windmill Theatre. But after a few months, there were complaints from the audience that I looked too young.

Some people thought I simply didn't look old enough to be at the Windmill. I was just barely 18, but I looked younger, and to some it was not proper that I was dancing in front of all those nudes.

I knew I would probably have to leave the Windmill, when one night, Van Damm called me into his office.

"I'm very sorry. I will have to let you go," he said. "But you will be welcomed back in a couple of years."

I was upset. I implored him to change his mind. "I'm trying to support my mother," I told him.

"I'll tell you what I'll do," he said. "You come in here every week and collect your salary, even though you are not working here. You can collect your salary until you find another show."

CHAPTER 9

My First Love

V an Damm suggested I see the lady in the office at the top of the theater, named Mrs. Beresford. She was the booking agent and knew what was going on in the theater world.

She acquired the comedy acts and other performers for the theater.

When I entered her office, I didn't pay much attention to the only other person in the room, a tall man, standing with his back to me.

"I think I have a job for you," Mrs. Beresford said.

"There's a pantomime called *Cinderella* and it's going on tour. The pantomime should run for about a month. As a matter of fact, the producer is right here," she said, turning to the man standing beside her.

As he turned around, I fell instantly in love with him.

He was tall, blond, in his early 20s, with perfect features. He had a beautiful smile. He was the most handsome man I've ever seen.

The booking agent introduced us.

"This is Mr. David Langhorne, of Langhorne productions. He's the producer," Mrs. Beresford said.

His blue eyes smiled back at me and in that instant I knew I'd have gone anywhere with him.

But I was just a kid. I'd never been in love before. Suddenly, I was in love with this man.

I joined the pantomime, hoping to see him often, but unfortunately for me he wasn't around that much. The pantomime was quite successful though, and I rode along on a wave of romantic imaginings.

Of course, David Langhorne never knew what I felt for him.

We toured for four weeks, and at one point I was asked to understudy *Cinderella*. Well, they never had a single understudy rehearsal. I never even saw a script.

One night in the depths of winter, the leading lady said, "Oh, I've got such a terrible sore throat. You may have to go on for me."

"Don't be ridiculous," I said. "I've never had a rehearsal; I've never even seen the script. You are just going to have to go ahead."

So she did.

We toured by train to various cities. It was awkward traveling, but we had a theater compartment on the train to take us from city to city where the pantomime was showing.

We never missed the train. We all had "train call" early in the mornings when we moved on to other cities, to make sure we didn't get left behind.

Our carriage had reserved signs on the windows to make sure we had seats. We all squeezed in. Of course, the props and scenery came in another part of the train, in the baggage compartment.

It was a nice little pantomime, and well-put together.

That first Christmas of the war was quiet; nothing much was happening. The air raids didn't start right away, not until France fell. Only once in a while would a Luftwaffe plane fly over England.

All the while, my heart ached to see David. He was attending a few rehearsals, but he wasn't really connected in a hands-on way. Another fellow was actually directing the show.

At each city where we toured, we stayed in what was called theater digs. Some women in the towns only rented rooms out to theater people. You had to contact them quickly and book yourself in because there weren't that many of them.

From the train we had to walk to our digs, carrying our heavy suitcases. I brought enough clothes for four weeks. It was difficult, but that's what you do when you're in a traveling show.

When we arrived at each new town's theater, we would search out the notice board with the listing of possible theater digs for the following week's location. I would write immediately, asking if they could accommodate two, because I stayed with another girl.

We looked for a letter back saying, "Yes we have a room for you." That way we knew where we would spend the night when we arrived in each new place. The postal service was always reliable.

Because this was during the war, we had to give the landladies our ration books, when we arrived at each new lodging house. They would feed us for a week. You'd get two meals: a breakfast and a meal after the show.

When *Cinderella* came to an end I was talking about David Langhorne with a girl who was in the show with me. I admitted to myself that I'd fallen head over heels in love with the producer. But of course, I couldn't tell her that.

Instead I asked, "Do you know if he's putting on any more shows?"

She asked a question in return. "Do you know what his real name is?"

"No," I said, surprised.

"It's Astor. He's David Astor, Lord Astor's son! The family may not know that he's in the theater business. Can you imagine that? Langhorne was his mother's maiden name. Before she married Lord Astor, she was Nancy Langhorne."

That was kind of a shock. I thought, "There goes my romance. I'm never going to get up to his standards and I'm no Cinderella."

So I gave up on him.

He didn't put on many shows after he produced *Cinderella*, as far as I know.

But a strange thing happened 40 years on, when I was married and living in the U.S.A., near Chicago.

* * *

The incident happened decades after my pantomime experiences, long after a U.S. Army Air Force officer had swept me off my feet and married me, and we had moved to Naperville, Illinois. A chance encounter shocked me and brought back a cascade of memories of the *Cinderella* incident.

It probably shocked David Astor as well.

It happened when I was invited one evening to attend a special event at Marshall Fields, in Chicago. Marshall Fields was one of America's most famous department stores located on State Street (that same great street that Frank Sinatra loved to sing about).

My aunt, who was into furnishings, worked for many years at Marshall Fields, in the Oxford Rooms that featured elegant furniture.

"We're having a special occasion tonight," she told me one day.

"Lord Astor, who owns Hever Castle in England, wants some furnishings from our Chicago store. After the store closes we are going to have a special occasion here. We'll have champagne and there will be a harpist to entertain. Of course, there will be refreshments and you can come as my guest," she said.

I didn't hesitate in accepting the invitation. I tried to imagine what David Astor would look like now, four decades after our encounter.

When the furniture showing concluded, we were all dutifully lined up in a reception room to be introduced to Lord Astor.

I longed to see the guest of honor. A harpist was playing soft background music, and waitresses were flitting around, handing out glasses of champagne and tasty *hors d' œuvres*.

But when the guest of honor arrived, he was not the same man I had fallen in love with many decades ago. He was much younger than "my" David Astor should have looked by now.

Later that evening, I approached him and asked him if he was related to David Astor.

"Of course," he replied. "He's my uncle."

"I worked for him once," I said.

"Really. Some sort of secretarial work?" he asked me.

"Oh no," I replied. "I was in one of his pantomimes. He put on Christmas pantomimes. As a matter of fact, I was in *Cinderella*."

He looked astonished. "My uncle produced pantomimes? I don't think any of the family knows about that! Am I going to tease him about that when I get back to England!" he said with a grin.

I crept away with my foot in my big mouth. Later on, I started to laugh, "Oh dear, poor David."

I didn't know my old heartthrob was trying to keep his involvement with the theater a total deep, dark secret from his family forever. I may never know why he did that.

I guess it is true that loose lips sink ships. Only I don't think any real harm was done by my revelation some 40 years after the fact.

CHAPTER 10

Put Out Those Lights!

E arly in 1940, there were still few signs of the intense bombings we were expecting, except a few air raids on some of the southern shipyards.

Auditions were being held for the pantomime, *Jack and Jill*, at the Palace Theater in London. Having made up my mind that I wanted to stay in London, I auditioned and managed to get into the production.

Usually pantomimes last about three weeks to a month. But we had so many stars in this show that it ran for four months, and then an encore for an extra two weeks.

Meanwhile, after some fierce air battles, Hitler was believed to be thinking that he had failed in his ability to destroy the RAF and our airfields, because our fliers were still in the skies. But his desire to invade Britain had not waned.

The British troops were in France and fighting the Nazi Regime, as Germany marched into country after country.

Denmark had been swallowed up; Norway was infiltrated by the Third Reich. Belgium also fell, and some 30,000 civilians were killed in Rotterdam, Holland by the Nazi invaders.

Because I was in the entertainment business, I was exempt from being called up into military service to defend the nation. Only a few professions, besides entertainment, were exempt, including police personnel, naturally.

However, we were all expected to do whatever might be necessary to help in the war effort and to report any suspicious activities.

We had to put up blackout materials on all windows in lieu of regular curtains, so lights inside the houses at night could not be seen by any enemy planes that might fly overhead. This, it was hoped, would confuse the bombers about the locations of their targets.

There was a dash to buy the special blackout material, when it was announced that we had to use it. It was required. No excuses.

Air raid wardens would come around at night, and if any chink of light showed through the windows from inside homes, they would let the residents know about it. "Put out those lights!" they would yell.

The old curtains were recycled quite successfully into clothing in most cases. I didn't do that myself. However, I did begin to wonder if perhaps I should have taken my Hollywood sewing classes a little more seriously. Still, the entertainment business kept me too busy for anything else.

Nothing was ever wasted in wartime, especially edible goods, which became scarce.

We ate out a lot. Spam was the main item on most menus. Long lines formed in all the restaurants and food snack bars. Queuing up for food became the norm.

Early in May, the two houses of the British Parliament voted "no confidence" in Prime Minister Neville Chamberlain, because before war was declared, he had signed a peace pact with Hitler.

Few people believed Hitler would keep his word. He didn't seem to know the meaning of the word "peace."

Personally, I think that Chamberlain probably recognized the terrible danger Adolf Hitler and his Nazi Regime posed to the rest of the world, and how unprepared we were. By signing the treaty, we made Hitler think we were not going to start defense, or war, preparations.

But actually, we were.

In any case, King George VI called in Winston Churchill to lead the nation on its perilous course to preserve freedom. At age 65, Churchill became prime minister and rallied the nation to withstand our deadly enemy.

I often heard him on the wireless giving encouraging speeches.

Also giving radio broadcasts, to help take our minds off our worries and keep our chins up, was C.S. Lewis, author of *The Great Divorce*, *The Screwtape Letters*, and the popular children's stories, *The Chronicles of Narnia*. The last is about the adventures of two brothers and their two sisters who were evacuated to a mysterious country house because of the war. Their curiosity about an old wardrobe took them into a strange and beautiful world called *Narnia*.

While speakers on radio programs served to keep us thinking positively, the news from abroad was not good.

The Maginot Line, near the boarder of France and Germany, fell apart at this time. Then the French capitulated and our troops found themselves fighting a rearguard action ending at Dunkirk on the northern coast of France.

Churchill went on the radio telling everybody who owned petrol-powered boats to rescue the men over on the beaches of Dunkirk, where the Germans had trapped our army.

He instructed the volunteers to leave all the equipment, get the men in the boats, and bring them back to England.

About 1,000 small vessels sailed that night across 40 miles of choppy, open sea in the English Channel to rescue some 300,000 soldiers of the British Expeditionary Force, and also some French, Polish and Belgian troops. The little civilian-owned boats were guided to the beaches of Dunkirk by a few Royal Navy destroyers.

But a lot of the little boats, including a pleasure steamboat like the one we entertained on during the summers with "The Mayfair Babes," were blown out of the water by the Germans. The Jerries were bombing and strafing the rescue boats from their positions near Dunkirk.

After about a week of valiant rescue efforts by the armada of small sea craft, it became clear that we had to totally re-equip the entire army. So we were entirely dependent at that time on our Royal Air Force to defend our island. We prayed that America would enter the war to come help us.

Hitler swore he would invade our little island.

Churchill vowed Hitler would never succeed.

"Never give in. Never give in. Never yield to the enemy," was his frequent battle cry.

The whole nation seemed to concur. The terror of the London Blitz was unimaginable and still several weeks away.

* * *

We had a great view of London from our flat in Piccadilly, because we were living on the top story of a four-story building. A little balcony came out from the kitchen and you could see all around the area from there.

One evening, my mother saw a curious sight, and called me over to the window.

"I was closing our blackout curtains when I saw a strange light," my mother told me as I came to the window.

"Look at that! Why is a light flashing? It's on another roof," she said, pointing to a building some distance away.

"It can't be a signal. It must be someone checking a battery on their torch," I surmised.

We didn't think any more of it and closed the curtains. But the next night my mother was looking out again. "You know that light is still flashing," she said.

"Maybe I should find a policeman and tell him," I said, and hurried down the four flights of stairs and into the street.

I was surprised to see a policeman was right there, on duty outside our building. So I told him what we had seen.

"Let me come up and take a look," he said.

We showed him into the kitchen and pointed out where the light was flashing.

"I'll go and report this at the local police station on Charing Cross Road," the policeman said.

I thought, "Well that's taken care of." But a few nights later we saw it again.

"That's very strange," my mother said, looking rather worried now.

We surmised that on a clear night, if a plane was coming in low it could see a light flashing somewhere on a building, and that could be a signal to guide it to its target.

"This time I'll go down to the police station and report it myself," I said.

I went down to the Charing Cross Road Police Station and asked to see a detective. I told him what we had observed.

"No policeman came and reported this to us," the chief detective said, looking grave.

"I think it's fair to assume he was bogus. In fact, he could well have been an Irishman posing as an English policeman. We get a lot of that," the inspector informed me.

That was scary.

The bogus law officer was right outside our front door, and we had even let him into our flat. And what was worse, the suspicious light was not reported by any "policeman."

There was no record of a bobby being on duty in front of our house that night. But they caught the pretender a few days later, standing in front of our building again, perhaps waiting to see if we were going to try to report the strange light.

But, after he was caught, the light was never seen again, and we were confident that whoever was doing it was apprehended.

A lot of curious things like that happened during the blackouts.

CHAPTER **11**

Let There Be Lights

T he possible ugly consequences of such mysterious occurrences didn't fully dawn on us.

There was a theory that there existed some kind of agreement that cities would not be bombed during wars. The fight would be between armies in the field and navies on the oceans.

What we didn't know was that the days of keeping cities off limits were over.

One night soon after the mysterious light incident, a single German airplane apparently got lost over London. The aircraft was loaded with bombs. The pilot probably didn't want to take them back to Germany unused, so he just dropped them.

That was the first time London was bombed in WWII.

It was an apparent navigational mistake of the bomber that set off a firestorm.

I don't know how many people died in that lone incident, but Prime Minister Winston Churchill was infuriated. The very next night he sent a whole RAF squadron over to Berlin, and lit up the whole place.

Berliners apparently thought they would never need blackout curtains to hide their city from our bombers. They never thought we would strike back.

How wrong they were!

By June 1940, after touring with a show called "Me and My Girl," I was again out of work.

But when my mother was talking to a friend (my mother had a lot of friends) she learned about a troupe of girls who were in a variety show called "Go To It."

They needed a replacement for one girl who had to leave the troupe. "Maybe Pauline could replace the girl that left," the friend suggested.

I was very happy to have a chance to work again. I auditioned right away, and was accepted.

The plan was that I would rehearse for a few days in London then join the company in Plymouth. Another girl in the variety show said that she would share theatrical digs with me.

It was all planned and we were excited. We were supposed to catch the train on Sunday morning to go down to the port of Plymouth, on the south coast. But unfortunately, this new friend said that she couldn't join me until Monday, because of sickness in the family.

So I went down to Plymouth on my own.

I found the theater digs quite easily. It was a large, two-story house. The husband and wife were very welcoming.

"We don't expect any air raids of course. But if there should be one, this is how you find your way to the shelter …" they said. They mentioned the names of several streets to use and where to turn left, and where to go right, to find the air raid shelter.

I was really tired after the train journey, and I was only half-listening. I thought, "That won't be necessary. There won't be any raids."

They gave me a meal, and I went to bed looking forward to being in the show the next evening.

During the night, I suddenly heard a lot of noise outside. Explosions were all around the house. For the moment I thought I was imagining things. I was only half awake.

I looked out the window. Searchlights were all over the sky and I thought, "My God it's an air raid!"

I ran downstairs. The landlord and landlady were nowhere to be found. They must have made a run for the air raid shelter, I thought.

I didn't know which way to go. I couldn't remember the names of any streets to take to get to the shelter! Even if I had remembered, with the noise going on outside it seemed highly improbable that I would have made it there alive.

I remembered reading something about if there is a closet under a staircase, if you get in there and if the house is bombed, you might survive.

I rushed downstairs. Fortunately, there was a closet there.

I pulled all the clothes off the pegs and put them on top of me. That's where I spent the rest of the night, thinking, "Well, this is the end of me."

The next morning, I was still alive and the landlady and her husband came prancing back.

"Thank goodness the house is still standing," they said.

I was thankful that I was still standing.

"It has been a very, very bad raid. This was the first bad raid on a city," the landlady informed me.

"There's no more electricity or water. Hundreds of people have been made homeless," she added.

To eat that day we had to go to a nearby school. They were opening up many schools for people to get relief, to shelter in, and to get some food.

I had breakfast in the school cafeteria. Then I thought maybe I should go down to the theater and see if anybody is there, and see whether the building is still standing.

When I got to the correct address, I saw that the theater had been spared, and the rest of the company was congregating there. But we weren't quite sure what to do. With no electricity for lighting, how could we put on a show?

"I'm going to get in touch with the mayor and ask what we should do," the stage manager said.

The mayor suggested that if we ask everybody who wants to come to the show to bring flashlights, and they all shine them onto the stage, maybe they might be able to see every bit of the show.

"The musicians can use candles and put them somehow

on their music stands, so they can see the music," the mayor of Plymouth said.

This is how we put on the show that night; it was a packed house. Everyone that came to see the show brought flashlights that they shone on the stage.

I had a solo tap dance in the show, and I was toward the front of the stage busy tapping away, when everyone started to laugh. I couldn't image why they were laughing.

When it was over I heard a voice behind me say, "Turn around."

There was a line of stagehands shining their flashlights on my feet while I was tapping. That was the reason for the laughter. The audience was delighted and amused at the same time. The applause was intense.

Unbeknownst to me, the morning following the terrible air raid, my mother was on a train with a friend going down to another town. Her friend was reading the newspaper as the train rattled along.

"Any news?" my mother asked.

"Oh, it's terrible. There's been an air raid on Plymouth and hundreds killed," the friend replied.

"Oh my God, Pauline is there!" said my mother, horrified.

She got off at the next station and caught the next train straight back to London.

She called up our dance director, but was unable to get through to anybody. My mother was absolutely panic-stricken. The telephone lines were down; communication with Plymouth was cut off. There was not even any transportation available to the town.

The Luftwaffe was apparently trying to hit the dockyards at His Majesty's Naval Base in Davenport, but the bombs had really hit hard at an area of Plymouth, called Swilly, instead. The name Swilly means "farmland." My theater digs were in that area.

The Jerries missed the base altogether, but I happened to be in the wrong place at the wrong time.

About two days later, the telephone lines were repaired and the dance director was able to get through to the company director in London. He said we were all saved and the show will go on.

I made up my mind then that when the tour ended, I would stay closer to home. I would not seek work outside London again.

Little Ballerina.

The Birthday Brownie.

Louisa Mabbett

Looking sweet for *Sweeter and Lower*.

Pinup girls, *Sweeter and Lower* (second edition).

Appearing with Hermione Gingold in *Sweet and Low* (first edition).

Outside Maj. Gen. James Doolittle's house in High Wickham.

The glamour of it all.

My wedding day, June 1945, (and my mother came too).

CHAPTER 12

Dark Nights

S till touring with the variety show "Go To It," we arrived in the ancient city of Bath.

Here, the famous novelist Jane Austen lived for a time, in the early 19th century gathering background for many of her much-loved novels, including *Persuasion* and *Northanger Abbey*.

She described the famous Grand Pump Room and the assembly rooms in her romances. Elegant people attended fashionable balls in the assembly rooms. The women dressed in long Empire-line gowns of silk and satin and wore long white gloves to the balls.

Almost two millennia earlier, the Romans had arrived. They made Bath into a spa and resort town with hot and cold baths created from natural mineral water springs. They built bathing houses and temples, and worshiped the pagan goddess Minerva.

Those seeking good health would come to Bath throughout the centuries and "take the waters," sometimes staying weeks, hoping to get better if they suffered from an ailment. Or, they would come just to take things easy and drink the waters of Bath expecting longevity—people still do that.

However, our experience in this town was not going to be so relaxing, although we did make a surprise visit to the bathhouses.

When we arrived in the city there was a horrific air raid going on. We couldn't find the street where our digs were located. So we went to the police station and told them we couldn't find the house where the landlady expected us to arrive that night.

"It's no use going out in this raid," the police officer told us.

"You'll have to spend the night somewhere. We'll open up the baths for you."

So they took us up to the baths and told us to put sheets on the massage tables and sleep on top of the tables. It seemed like our only choice. So we took off just our outer clothes and climbed up on the massage tables to sleep. We slept pretty well.

But the next morning we were awakened by noises of all kinds. The baths were open and people were coming in. One fellow came in to where we were waking up and just stood and stared at us in utter surprise.

We quickly dressed as more startled people came in and looked at us. Then we went trudging out with our suitcases, trying to look as normal as possible.

We found our digs later that day. But our trip to the bathhouses was unforgettable.

I later learned that an ancient legend has it that if a Roman had his clothes stolen at the baths, he would write a curse on a stone tablet to be read by the goddess Minerva. The wronged Roman would expect punishment to ensue for the perpetrator.

Fortunately, we didn't have our clothes stolen while we were there. That was lucky for us, but even luckier for any would-be thief. He'd never have gotten away with that.

* * *

When the tour was over, I went back to our apartment on Broad Court.

It was good to be home again. Of course, invasion was an ever-present possibility, even though England had not been invaded since 1066 when the Normans crossed the English Channel, and, although they weren't welcome, they stayed.

We could hardly think what it would be like if we were invaded by an enemy force.

Music took our minds off the impending danger. During the evenings, when my father was at home, he would play his violin to practice and to try to entertain us. I spent hours listening to him play. Sometimes it drove me crazy, but he was a brilliant violinist, so I could hardly complain.

My father often invited opera stars to our apartment; they would come over and start practicing. He would play the piano for them when they wanted coaching with certain arias. He knew the arrangements well, because he would be conducting the orchestra for their operatic performances. He could play anything, but he couldn't sing a tune to save his life.

My father actually could have been a concert pianist, because he played so well, but he had short arms. That works against you when you want to be a concert pianist. Short arms run in the family. I inherited them, unlike my mother's; she had long limbs.

She was tall and elegant. By the time I was born, she had her hair colored dark, and was wearing it in a bob, as was the style in 1920s. But when my mother was a teenager, and even as a young woman living in Canada, her hair was its natural blonde color and her tresses hung down below her waist. Her hair was so long she could sit on it.

One summer evening in 1940, when the war was heating up, my mother and I were home alone, and she was cooking in the kitchen, when Prime Minister Winston Churchill spoke on the radio. His famous speech was being broadcasted about how we would all fight with anything and everything in our power to stop the aggressors, if they dared to invade our homeland.

His voice came across the airwaves in his heavy, guttural, determined "growl" that had become so familiar to the British people: "… We shall defend our island, whatever the cost may be. We shall fight on the beaches. We shall fight on the landing grounds. We shall fight in the fields and in the streets. We shall fight in the hills. We shall never surrender!"

My mother stopped what she was doing, looked at me doubtfully and said, sarcastically, "Oh yer … oh fine."

But I was really flustered by the possibility.

"What will we do if the Germans invade England? What are we going to do?" I asked her. "Supposing the Germans do land and they march down Charing Cross Road, and come up here and knock on the door?"

She went to the kitchen counter and pulled out a drawer and took out two sharp knives.

"I've got two knives here, one for you and one for me," she said. "If they come through that door we get as many as we can."

I felt relieved knowing what I was supposed to do. I felt better knowing there was a plan, even if it could have ended in a blood bath. The plan was that I was to knife as many Nazis as I can, and get it over with quickly. Luckily, I didn't have to do that.

My mother was always full of solutions. She always seemed to be ready for anything, even the strong possibility of invading Nazis.

The Battle of Britain raged in the skies over our heads during that summer of 1940, as our outnumbered RAF fighter plane pilots made valiant attempts to stop the German Luftwaffe. By September, the Blitz was upon us, but the Germans had found that our RAF was too difficult to destroy, so they redirected their invasion plans to Russia.

Even so, London was bombed every night during the Blitz; I don't know how we survived. I only know that the idea of actually surrendering never entered our minds. That would have been unthinkable!

Our first official air raid shelter was at Russell's Department Store—no relation to my uncle Alec Russell. If we were at home when the sirens started to sound, signaling the alarm, we would rush over to the store and into the basement as quickly as possible. It was a big general merchandise shop, and the basement was huge. We were allowed to sleep in the aisles. About 60 or 70 people were sleeping between the aisles on an average night, because the raids came nightly during the Blitz.

One night at about 2 a.m., when my father was home with us for a change, and not conducting, we all were in the department store basement and could hear the whistle of the bombs coming down—then a deathly silence for a moment.

Suddenly, there was a huge explosion. The whole place shook. Plaster fell down from the ceiling and a few people screamed.

For a minute I thought we'd been hit.

But the real damage happened across the street where 200 debutantes were having a dance in what they thought was a safe place, because it was an underground nightclub.

The debutantes had just come from a ball at Buckingham Palace and they were continuing their special night out at Café de Paris.

It was the underground club where—when the raids first started—we had made our unexpected arrival, clutching pillows and blankets, dressed in our pajamas, mistakenly thinking that the fancy nightclub was our designated air raid shelter.

Far beneath the streets of London, the debutantes were having a grand time on the dance floor, when an aerial torpedo bomb went straight down the elevator shaft and exploded right on the dance floor.

That was the massive explosion we heard as we huddled

in the basement of Russell's Department Store. All 200 debutantes and their dates were killed.

Help was greatly needed and an air raid warden rushed into our basement, making a hurried announcement.

"Will all able-bodied men please come with me at once!" he yelled.

My father went of course, to see what could be done to help the victims.

He was gone a couple of hours, but we weren't really worried about him. When he returned, he was shaking and as white as a sheet; I had never seen him look so pale.

After he caught his breath he just stared at the floor and said, "I have never had to pull so many dead bodies out of a building before."

The only ones who survived the direct hit inside the Café de Paris, were the floor show girls who were in the dressing rooms at the time. A circular tunnel ran around the perimeter of the dance floor and the tunnel area was made into dressing rooms. That's what saved them.

One of the girls was a very good friend of mine. I was so happy to see her, and know that she came out of that horrendous scene alive. As she came to take cover with us, she confirmed that all the floor show girls were spared.

"A few of us were cut by flying glass, but none of us were seriously injured. If we had started performing ten minutes sooner, we would have been killed too," she told me, her voice trembling.

But the band was wiped out. Every member of the band was killed that terrible night. Their musical talent was silenced forever.

My friend told me the graphic details of the bombing: the deafening explosion, the screams, and the mangled dead bodies. The fright suffered by the survivors would be repeated in their nightmares for months after the event.

And the bombing put an end to the annual debutante balls for rest of the war.

A few nights later, when the air raid sirens started wailing, we hurriedly grabbed what bedding we could carry with us, and went down to the shelter. London was once again being pummeled; it was a bad, bad raid.

When it was all over, we came up to street level. It was still dark as we started to go home, but we were stopped in our tracks by a yellow police ribbon all around our street.

I asked a policeman what was going on.

"You can't see from here," he said. "But if you come around this side of your house you can see the damage. The windows are blown out and there's a huge crack from the top of the building all the way down the side of the house. I suggest you look for somewhere else to live, because if they drop another bomb nearby, the whole building will collapse," the policeman said.

So we paid a visit to the London housing authority and asked for accommodations.

All they could find for us was a little two-room flat. It wasn't too bad and it was in the same building as some of the police station offices, so we felt safe there.

CHAPTER 13

The Yanks Are Coming!

With our new apartment we were assigned to a different air raid shelter. This one was located in the basement of London's main Masonic Lodge.

I remember running home at night through the streets, with my hands over my head for protection from the smoldering debris that was falling from burning buildings.

I ran as fast as I could during the raids, jumping over holes in the pavement, trying to get to the shelter.

Finally, when I reached the door I would throw myself inside and down the stairs into the basement. It felt like I was running in an obstacle course.

My mother was always there, waiting for me. She kept our place, spreading out blankets and pillows between the filing cabinets. I would fall onto the blankets and try to catch my breath.

The whole building was made of huge slabs of marble. If we were hit, I was sure we would be buried alive, and they would never be able to dig us out.

But miraculously, that didn't happen, and we made it back to our home alive every morning.

One December day in 1941, as soon as I woke up, I saw my mother listening intently to the wireless.

"Pearl Harbor has been bombed," she said.

"What's a pearl harbor?" I asked, sleepily. I pictured a string of pearls, and a harbor where pearl earrings or rings, or some such things are made.

Like most people in Britain I had no idea what, or where, Pearl Harbor was.

"It is somewhere in America," my mother replied. "This is good news, because now the United States will enter the war."

Not long after that, many U.S. military personnel began to arrive in Great Britain and help in the struggle against Hitler. Simultaneously, the American forces also were preparing to react to Japan's terrible surprise bombing of Pearl Harbor, Hawaii. The attack destroyed much of the American Naval fleet and killed 2,335 U.S. servicemen.

That attack caused the United States to enter World War II.

A few days after Pearl Harbor, the Japanese attacked Hong Kong. At that time, Hong Kong was a British crown colony.

The Americans that came to England first, were mostly U.S. Army Air Force personnel. Some volunteer pilots had actually arrived before the war started, and joined up with the Royal Air Force. They wore smart, dark blue uniforms and called themselves the Eagle Squadron.

About 300 pilots from the United States arrived in England before the war to fly the fighter planes. The Eagle Squadron had their headquarters very close to where I lived. Unfortunately, at the end of the war, there was only one survivor out of the original 300 volunteer airmen.

Even after the start of the war, we had no bases for the Americans' planes. They had to build everything from scratch, taking over farms, plowing the fields and laying down runways.

Nissen huts, made of prefabricated steel were put up for them to live in. The Yanks were literally building small towns.

I didn't know him at the time, but my future husband was stationed at a base in Norfolk. He was with the 392nd bomber group. From there, Flying Fortresses would take off and fly mainly on daylight raids over Germany.

Unfortunately, fighter planes could not accompany the Flying Fortresses all the way into Germany; they did not have enough fuel capacity or range. So the Flying Fortresses would have to continue flying on their own, without the protection of the fighter planes.

They would fly in very close formation, and, after the war I was told by one pilot, they lost quite a few planes that collided into each other, which was a tragedy.

My husband told me later that they would send up 27 bombers, or Fortresses, and they would be lucky if 16 came back.

The losses were terrible, until finally they equipped the P-51 Mustangs with enough fuel to accommodate their flights into Germany. Then, with the agile Mustangs accompanying the bombers, the losses of the bombers went way down and they were able to complete their missions.

One benefit of having the Americans in England is that they increased our rations. Everyone was issued an extra can of Spam per month, and also a tin of powdered eggs.

Potatoes were not rationed; they were homegrown throughout the nation. My mother became very good at making potato pancakes.

Mostly, we bought special bread, made from a government-developed recipe. It was supposed to be very healthy for us. It must have been pretty good, because we actually never got sick, except for an occasional cold or case of the flu, in which case we still had to perform. The show would always go on!

Clothing was rationed, of course. We only had a few coupons per month, about 27 in each ration book. Everything we needed to wear had to be bought with coupons, including shoes.

Naturally, a black market arose where little men with large suitcases would come along, offering clothing—coupon free—but at rather high prices.

Curtains and upholstery material were not rationed. So we became rather clever at making dresses, suits and coats out of what suitable material we could find, including, of course, all kinds of curtain material.

* * *

The fight in the Pacific was now on in earnest, so we were truly in a worldwide war. Tragically, this was the second time a world war had occurred in the 20th Century. All nations were involved in the fighting in one way or another.

Besides fighting the enemy, the U.S. soldiers, sailors and airmen, who continued to pour into England, were very good to the children of the United Kingdom. They gave them candy and sweets; they played with them and put on Christmas parties and birthday parties, trying to keep their spirits up.

But most of all, the presence of the American military meant we had even more confidence that with their help we would prevail in the struggle against Hitler.

Now, all the difficulties, the bombings, the rationing of clothes and food, didn't seem to matter so much, because we were sure we would win this terrible war.

CHAPTER 14

The Spy Catcher

In the spring of 1942, I went to meet a friend for lunch. She was working at The Cabaret Club on Beak Street. That was not too far from my home. It was a private club that had a very good floor show. She suggested I go along to the club to audition as a dancer.

My friend said that the Cabaret Club has a very small dance floor and that's why they really want smaller girls. So I packed up my tap shoes and off I went.

I showed them some of my American tap dancing routines. The director seemed very pleased with it; I must have given a good audition.

"We are paying the girls four pounds a week. If you do a solo, we will pay you more," the director said.

That sounded good to me and I agreed to work there.

We performed in the shows at 10 p.m. and 1 a.m. Members

of the club were seated under soft lighting at round tables spread with crisp white tablecloths, while they watched the floor show. It was a very intimate venue.

Soon, I had a solo spot. I was dancing in the spotlight by myself, and singing, accompanied by the club orchestra. My first solo was danced to some lively Latin American music. I wore a cargo hat, and a white velvet pantsuit that was custom made for me. It had a little bolero jacket covered in sequins that sparkled brilliantly under the spotlight with every tap of my feet.

Mr. Murray, who ran the club, had very strict rules. He reminded me of Van Damm in that respect. Some hostesses were employed to sit with customers, but he stressed we dancers were not allowed to do that.

"None of the dancers are ever to mingle with the customers. Between shows, dancers can go out and have a meal and come back. Otherwise, you must stay in your dressing room," Mr. Murray said.

We had some very well-known people who were members of the club, including Prince Bertil of Sweden. He used to come in frequently, always with his *aide-de-camp*. Like so many other leaders of European countries that were now under the iron rod of the Nazis, the prince had apparently taken refuge in London.

Mr. Murray bent his "no mingling" rule for Prince Bertil, who asked him if any of the dancers in the show could sit with him and have dinner—one girl volunteered.

Then, the dance director's wife, who was also in the floor show, said, "Maybe Pauline could go with you."

Of course, being very thrilled, I accepted the invitation.

The prince was such an extremely good-looking man, tall and dark-haired. He spoke almost perfect English, which was good because I didn't speak Swedish. He always traveled with his *aide-de-camp*. I believe he was attached to the Swedish Navy and I assumed he was working at the Swedish Embassy in London. He came to the Cabaret Club at least once or twice a month.

Although at that time we had strict food rationing in Britain, we were served steaks for dinner whenever the Prince came into the club. That was a thrill not only because it was something special to dine with a prince, but also because dancing made us hungry.

The Cabaret Club's last show of the night did not finish until about 2:30 a.m. So most nights my mother would walk all the way from Charing Cross Road to the club. She wanted to walk home with me after the show, to make sure I made it safely back to our flat.

She came out even during some of the worst air raids. I don't know how she had the courage to walk to the theater that late at night as buildings were being bombed all over the place. It was difficult to see even the roadway. The bright lights of the city, indicating such places as theaters, police stations, and hospitals were turned off as a safety precaution against aerial raiders.

Lights in the shop windows were specially designed to show only a dim blue color so that they could not be seen from the air by enemy aircraft. Most were placed all around the shop windows, but they were hardly enough to light a pedestrian's way through the rubble-strewn streets.

Vehicles also had to have the dim blue lights installed, in lieu of headlights. All the traffic moved very slowly, and there were few traffic accidents.

Once in a while, if a raid was heavy, when we were coming home from the nightclub, we had to duck into a shop doorway. My mother wasn't one to go into shelters too much.

When she was a young woman during World War I, the Germans conducted the zeppelin aerial raids on London, and she got through that. I think she must have had a feeling that she would survive this war as well, because she wasn't nearly as nervous as I was.

One night, though, when a raid was particularly bad, I had to walk home by myself. As I felt my way through the darkened streets, a young American GI approached me. I could tell at once he had had a little too much to drink.

At first I thought, I should make a run for it. But I didn't know what his reaction would be. I thought, he might chase me and that wouldn't be good. So I kept walking.

He insisted on escorting me and hanging on my arm. I knew he wouldn't harm me in any way. I believed the best thing to do was just keep talking to him until I got to Charing Cross Road.

During the blackout, you couldn't tell one building from another. In this particular situation that was an asset.

"Why don't you go off and do whatever you want to do?" I urged the GI.

"Oh come along now," he insisted. "You can take me home with you, and I can sleep this off."

I thought it is no good arguing with him or trying to make him go back to his barracks by himself. So I kept on talking to him. But instead of taking him to my building, I took him to the building across the street from where I lived.

He didn't know which building he was in front of because of the blackout; no signs were lit up to indicate which building we were near.

"Is this where you live?" he asked me, slurring his words.

"Yes, this is where I live. You just have to go up the steps and open those doors," I said, pointing to the double front doors.

He went up the steps and opened the doors and found himself in the local police station. I've never seen such a surprised look on anyone's face. I followed the GI in and told the sergeant what had happened.

"He meant no harm. He just has had too much to drink," I explained.

"Well then, we will either call an MP, or let him sleep it off, and then send him on his way," the officer assured me.

I hurried back to my flat across the street and I never saw that GI again.

It's a funny thing really, but there was very little crime in London during the war. People could walk around in the dark and you would feel pretty safe, from criminal activity at least. That's something you could never do today.

I think people were too concerned with staying alive and not getting hit by a bomb, or flying concrete, or glass from an exploding building.

A big danger was the possibility of falling into a crater left by the last night's raid. In some places, bombs had made huge holes in the road and sidewalks. Cars, street signs and even double-decker busses had fallen into the craters. Almost everybody carried flashlights, which we called torches, to light their way along the obstacle courses.

Crime was almost unheard of, and there was definitely no time for playing around.

* * *

One evening at the Cabaret Club, Mr. Murray came up to me before we started the show and posed a surprising question.

"How much time did you spend in America?" he asked.

I thought this question was a little bit odd. He had never really been interested before.

"I was there for two years as a teenager. I went to school and saw the country—from a Greyhound bus," I replied.

He seemed satisfied with that answer.

"I would like you to meet a gentleman who might be interested in talking to you," he said.

I didn't think any more about it, until two or three weeks later, when Mr. Murray called me into his office. That's when my life took a turn to the clandestine.

"I'm going to take you to meet a gentleman. You can sit at his table and have coffee with him. I want you to tell him about your experiences in America," he said.

I was curious, so I agreed.

He introduced me to an elderly English man. He was tall and gray-haired, and he was very charming.

I believed Mr. Murray to be always very protective and straightforward about things—like who to mingle with, and who to avoid—so I knew he wouldn't send me to meet someone inappropriate, or get involved with something that wasn't right.

The old gentleman invited me to sit at a table in the club and have coffee with him. If Mr. Murray approved, I thought to myself, "Then it should be all right to meet with this stranger."

We chatted for a while. Then my new acquaintance asked me a lot of questions about America—I wondered why. But still, because this was Mr. Murray's arrangement, I answered his questions frankly and without any qualms.

"I work for the government," he explained. "You might be useful to us in some way."

He didn't say which department he was with. I figured it was some sort of secret service agency, British intelligence, or an offshoot or something; perhaps it would be better not to ask.

"There are people over here, in London, posing as Americans who have never been to the States. They are posing as such. Maybe you, having been there, could tell right away if they really are Americans or not," he said.

He explained that they may just be young people pretending to be Americans, or young men showing off, or they may have some more sinister ideas. They could be enemy spies.

I thought, "Oh, what fun."

It never occurred to me that it might be dangerous. I never really gave espionage much thought, except when I went to see movies and when I had appeared in the Alfred Hitchcock film, *Sabotage*, when I was 12 years old.

I didn't want to think about what happens to people who get caught by the enemy in that kind of profession. So I pushed any thought of torture, hanging, or a firing squad to the back of my mind.

We chatted some more and I told him I would like to help. Then I had to leave him to get ready for the next show. When we came out onto the floor and started performing the show, he was gone.

As the weeks went by, I only met one man who was posing as an American. I could tell right away he'd never been to the United States.

It happened one evening, when I was on a double date and the other girl's date started talking about owning a munitions factory in the United States. It was obvious to me by the things he was saying that he was not a munitions expert and not an American. I was sure he was a fake.

He didn't seem to know about the country. He seemed to have a lot of money, yet he was a civilian.

Talk of such a factory reminded me of the munitions factory that had been in Grantham for many years. But I kept "mum" about that.

The gentleman with the government had told me that if I had any suspicions about anybody to report it right away to the inspector at the Bow Street Police Station.

So, as soon as I could, I visited with the inspector and mentioned to him about the conversation with my friend's date.

"See if you can see him a couple of more times and get more information," he said.

I went on a few more dates and got talking to him. I was still suspicious of his true identity.

Soon after that, Mr. Murray came to me between shows and said that the elderly gentleman I talked to before, would like to see me again. "I want you to go to see him and just talk to him about this. You can go before the next show starts," Mr. Murray said.

"A car will call for you at 11:30 p.m.," he assured me. "This time, you'll be going to the gentleman's office."

In the two-hour break between the shows that night, I quickly changed into my street clothes, but I didn't have time to take off my stage makeup.

The black, unmarked car arrived right on time and whisked me off to a large house in the Kensington area of London. We hadn't driven very far when we went through some imposing iron gates that swung open for us as we approached.

Once inside the house, a male servant showed me into a very beautiful drawing room.

I should mention that I had never told any of this to my mother. She had no idea what I was involved with, but at this point I was wondering if perhaps I should let her know what was going on.

Within a few minutes, a young man came into the drawing room, and asked me to follow him. I was shown into a large, opulent library.

The old gentleman was sitting there and he thanked me

for the information that I had forwarded to him, via the Bow Street Police Station detective. I was offered coffee and we chatted for quite a while about my experience in America, my schooling there and where I had traveled.

Then he asked me about my suspicions.

"I hope you will keep working for us. Would you be interested in continuing to observe these things for us?" he asked.

He hoped I would, he said, because there were so very few girls my age that had been to Hollywood and lived in the United States, who had a certain amount of education there, and, most importantly, who could identify an imposter. That could be helpful to the government, he said.

I agreed.

I thought it might work, because we met all kinds of people at other clubs we visited, when we had time. Occasionally, if we had a couple of hours between shows, we would go to other night clubs, just to see what they were doing in their floor shows, I explained. So we would meet a lot of people and get to talk to them.

I was ready to do my bit; although I was still in the dark as to what department that polite old gentleman was actually with.

When I left, I felt the time had come to tell my mother. So I did, as soon as I got home that night.

She had very firm feelings about it.

"You will not get involved in any kind of spy business," she stated.

"From now on you don't know anyone from anywhere. Who do you think you are, Mata Hari? You know what happened to her!"

CHAPTER 15

A Change of Scenery

S o, that was the end of my secret life with spies. I had to tell
Mr. Murray that I couldn't meet with the old gentleman
again, and I couldn't do the "work" he asked of me.

Although that was the end of that, I did hear an interesting
tidbit after the war was over, from a girl who still worked
at the Cabaret Club. She said that she saw something in
the newspaper about Mr. Murray being honored for doing
something for the government, during the war.

I pretended to be surprised.

When I was still working at the Cabaret Club early in
1943, my mother was getting work wherever she could. A
friend asked her one day what she was doing currently. After
all, she was no "spring chicken." She was now in her 50s.

"Oh, I'm with the Russian Ballet in Covent Garden now,"
she replied.

Her friend looked a little startled.

My mother didn't really look like a ballerina. For someone of her age—who had never had a dancing lesson—well, the friend just couldn't believe it.

But it was true.

The ballet company used to hire many extras every year for the big performances in the opera house at Covent Garden. They needed people to be swaying to the music in front of props designed like flower stalls and carts and large baskets of vegetables.

They had two or three major ballet productions each year; my mother appeared in the ballets for about three seasons.

Covent Garden, as the name suggests, was an area of London where fruits, vegetables and flowers were sold. The area was made famous by the colorful, 1964 musical *My Fair Lady*, starring Audrey Hepburn and Rex Harrison. (The movie was based on a play by George Bernard Shaw called *Pygmalion* which was written in 1912.)

My mother's life had always been colorful. In the early 1900s, she was living in Canada. She was a very adventurous woman, and always wanted to travel.

My grandfather was infected by wanderlust too. When he was a young man, he took off for Australia, leaving my grandmother and their four children in Grantham. He made, and lost, a couple of fortunes down under.

Then he came back to England. Lucky for him, my grandmother was in a forgiving mood; when he returned, she took him back into the family fold.

So, when his daughter said she wanted to go to Canada

at age 16, he gave her the money for her fare to sail over there, without any protest. She attended the Agriculture College in Winnipeg, Manitoba, and waited on tables to pay her tuition.

At the age of 17, my mother married a British man who was living in Canada. He worked with the Native Indians and used to go hunting wild animals. While he was out with his hunting parties, she would live in Indian villages eating around campfires and learning their crafts.

When her husband was out hunting in the wilderness one day, he was thrown from his horse and killed. She was pregnant at the time with a baby boy. Tragically, when she heard of her husband's death, she went into shock and lost the baby.

There was nothing to do then but return to England, where she soon got her first experience of war's impact on a civilian population: the zeppelin air raids on London. Apparently those air raids didn't faze her.

The Great War (1914 to 1918) also took many men's lives on the battlefields of France and Germany.

By then, my mother had secured a position at Daly's Theatre as an assistant manageress.

After that war, my father was conducting the orchestra for shows at the theater. That's when my parents met. They married and I came along a couple of years later.

During the time that my father was conducting the orchestra, the theater also presented the famous opera, *The Miracle*, a stunning depiction of the life of Christ.

Lady Diana Manners starred in that production. My

father became quite good friends with Lady Manners, whose family, the Rutlands, own Belvoir Castle where she lived as a child. The castle has been her family's ancestral home for about 500 years.

It is a coincidence that as a child, my mother played at the home of one her uncles, Uncle Rubin, who happened to work as a secretary for the Duke of Rutland at Belvoir Castle.

Uncle Rubin had a house on the Belvoir estate. He and his wife had no children, so he used to send a pony and trap to Grantham and pick up my mother and her two sisters, so they could play at the estate with the duke's children.

Everyone called the place Beaver Castle, which was much easier to pronounce than Belvoir Castle.

My mother and aunts went there during their summer holidays (the annual summer vacation for school children that at that time lasted about two months). For most children, it was a time of great escape and often a time for adventures.

The children of the castle (which we learned was built by one of the Norman invaders a thousand years before) and the children of the staff all played together on the grounds.

So it was quite a coincidence that my father, years later, began working with Lady Manners, who had been my mother's childhood playmate.

Life seems full of coincidences, although some people would say there are no such things.

When my father was in the British Army, before he met my mother, he suffered long-term injuries. He was "invalided out" of World War I, after he was wounded by poison gas.

Many, many hundreds of thousands of men suffered the same injuries.

He continued to have nasal problems after that war and finally decided to see a doctor.

He said that the doctor told him that if he started smoking it might help him with his nasal problems.

Of course, it didn't.

I suppose doctors in those days tried many different treatments!

My father used to buy cigarettes, but he really didn't want to smoke them.

It was perhaps the search of a better climate for breathing that prompted my father to take off—when I was about six years old—to tour India with the Carl Rosa Opera Company.

I don't think it helped his nasal problems much, although the spicy food may have had an impact.

* * *

During the Second World War, we lived in the Covent Garden area where the fresh market business was greatly hindered by the bombing. It was mostly a fruit and vegetable wholesale market by then. Men still moved some produce around in big baskets on their heads, but the war really curtailed that whole activity.

Fruit and vegetables became very hard to find; bananas were unheard of in England during World War II. Often, precious food supplies being sent over to us from the United States in ships, ended up at the bottom of the Atlantic Ocean after German submarines torpedoed the vessels.

Food that could be produced at home in England was brought into the city to be sold in makeshift food stalls, set up among the bombed out London streets and crumpled buildings. That helped provide food for people who lost their homes and places of employment in the air raids, and also helped to feed the rescue workers who assisted them.

The Covent Garden area, of course, was also very well known for cultural events and it still is. Ballets and operas are performed in the Royal Opera House. That building is actually referred to as Covent Garden. The original use of the site was for a garden for Westminster Abbey, in the 13th century.

But during the Blitz, the location, like almost all of London, was ablaze of fire every night.

Sometimes we heard of signs of hope in the midst of the madness of war. One such incident happened after the great London Cathedral, St. Paul's, took a bomb through the roof of the nave. The hole it left was really the only serious damage. Most of the structure, designed by the famous 17th century architect and astronomer, Sir Christopher Wren, was safe.

All around the cathedral, the heart of London was smoldering rubble. But the people were really startled to learn that flowers began to grow up around the sides of the cathedral, where none had grown before. The newspapers reported the phenomenon, which shocked some people and gave encouragement to many others. It seemed to be a sign that someone "up there" was watching over us.

And there were many heroes among the people; some

were very young. I remember seeing little children dragging along sacks filled with sand to smother fires that the bombs had set.

Some residents of the city went from living in big homes to living in hovels overnight. They had no choice. Even Buckingham Palace was bombed.

When buildings received only minor damage, it took only about a week sometimes to put doors and windows back into place so people would return to their homes or offices.

While I was still employed at the Cabaret Club, I got a phone call at home from a very dear friend who had auditioned at the Ambassadors Theatre a few days before.

"A new show is being produced," she said. "It's called *Sweet and Low*, and will star the famous comedienne and actress, Hermione Gingold."

My friend had auditioned, but was not accepted for the show.

"Why don't you go, Pauline, and try?" she asked. "You have more stage experience than I have. Maybe the position is still open."

I thought this would be a great chance for me to get back into the theater. As much as I loved performing at the Cabaret Club, and eating the steak dinners with Prince Bertil, I did miss the thrill of waiting for the curtain to rise, and the delightful feeling of smiling back at a theater's full house, as the audience gave us a standing ovation at the end of each show.

So I said good-bye to my friends at the Cabaret Club, and went over to the Ambassadors Theatre and auditioned.

The ballet mistress seemed pleased with me, and told me I would have to go and see the owner of the theater, Mr. Pemberton, who was also the producer of the show.

His office was up a long flight of stairs.

I introduced myself to his secretary, Irene Halfpenny, who sat at a desk in an outer office and appeared to me to be a very nice person.

"Mr. Pemberton will see you in a few minutes," she said.

It was more than a few minutes. But finally, I was called into his office; he invited me to sit down.

"The ballet mistress seems quite satisfied with you. She will be doing the choreography. Tell me about your experience," said the tall, kindly looking, middle-aged man.

I gave him a rundown of my theatrical, film, radio and dancing experiences.

"Now I want to see how you look," Mr. Pemberton said.

As I was sitting across the desk from him I thought, "Well, he can see how I look, so what does he mean?"

"Come and sit in this chair by me here," he instructed.

So I did, and he brought out a huge magnifying glass and put it right in front of my face. I suddenly froze and became extremely nervous wondering exactly what would happen next.

"Now, I have to peer through this and look at you," he said.

He peered through this magnifying glass and by that time I thought he must be some sort of pervert.

At this point, I was about to run out of the office. But I was still paralyzed with fear.

"Yes my dear, I think you will do very well," he said, moving the magnifying glass away from my face.

Trembling, I went quickly back to the outer office and explained to Miss Halfpenny what had happened.

She laughed.

"I should have told you before you went in that Mr. Pemberton is partially blind. The only way he could see how you look is through that magnifying glass. But I think you can say that you have the job," she said with a smile.

CHAPTER 16

The Adjutant's Office

The Ambassadors Theatre on West Street, in the Cambridge Circus area, had a very small company with only nine of us in the show. It was an intimate revue, with dancing, sketches, and monologues, and, of course, Hermione Gingold—that brilliant comedienne as the center of attention.

We were all fitted for costumes made mostly of satin and netting. For one show I wore what looked like only a big, tiger skin muff. I also had on long black gloves and a pearl necklace. But hidden by the muff, which I held in front of me, I was wearing gold lamé bra and panties.

With two of the other girls, Jackie and Mary, I performed a very funny sketch, which was especially designed to entertain the troops in the audience.

We rehearsed constantly, and at the dress rehearsal all the performers got a chance to sit in the audience and watch the other acts. As we came onstage, I could see Hermione Gingold was in the audience with Mr. Pemberton and several others, including Charles Hickman, the director.

Mary, Jackie and I began our monologue for the piece called "Pinup Girls." The chant went: "Cheering the boys who are winning the war, that's what pin-up girls are for."

It was a spoof on actual pinup girl pictures that aviators liked to put on the fuselage of their planes. And, what soldiers and sailors liked to paste up on the walls besides their beds and hammocks, to take their minds off what might be waiting for them the very next day.

We three girls were billed as "The Wall Flowers," even though we didn't look very much like wallflowers!

When it was my turn to say my piece after the other two girls, I walked forward, holding my muff firmly in place with my elegant, long black gloves.

Then, as part of the monologue I recited:

> I am made of more popular stuff,
> With a come hither look and a tiger skin muff.
> I move in high circles, although I'm a novice.
> I'm usually found in the adjutant's office.

When I said, "adjutant's office" I would take my hands away from the muff, but it would stay in place, because what the audience didn't know is that it was pinned to my brazier and there it would stay.

Everyone expected it to drop. That probably got the biggest laugh in the whole show.

At the dress rehearsal, Gingold found it hilarious.

I was glad about that because she had plenty to say about the shows that were produced. When she met someone for the first time, she would either like him or her a lot, or take an instant dislike to that person—and never want to see him or her again. For some people it was rejection at first sight for no apparent reason that we could figure out.

You would be fearful and trembling when you first met her, in case she wouldn't like you. If she didn't like you, you weren't out of the show, because you were under contract. But, if someone didn't meet with her approval it could be rather unpleasant.

I was one of the lucky ones; she approved of me. So I stayed in the show with her full support.

We were so successful that the show was presented for three years. The first edition of the show was in 1943, and was called *Sweet and Low*. In the second year that the production ran, 1944, the show was called *Sweeter and Lower*, and in the third year, 1945, it was called *Sweetest and Lowest*.

I was delighted to have my name mentioned on the billboard and programs with such stars as Gingold, also Henry Kendall, Walter Crisham, Ilena Sylva and Edna Wood.

Every night we would get big laughs. That's what audiences needed during the war.

And, we'd get fantastic reviews the next day in the newspapers. We were called, "Brilliantly caustic and comic ... charmingly dressed ... first rate entertainment, and brilliantly malicious."

The show was definitely a great hit, and we were on a roll.

* * *

I was soon chosen to understudy the principals. By that time I was earning eight pounds a week, and paid extra if I had to go on as an understudy.

Now, it was my mother's greatest desire that before she died, she would see me perform alone on the London stage.

That chance came and lasted one week, when the leading lady of the show took a vacation.

I wore a long, royal blue velvet dress with gathering across the bodice, and a wide sweetheart neckline. The leading lady wore it normally, but I was able to use it that whole week she was gone. However, the girl whose place I was taking was rather big-breasted, which may have been why the front was gathered into pleats. The bodice was much too big for me.

"I know what to do," said the wardrobe mistress. "I'll get some cotton wool and we'll stuff it down the front."

That's how I had to go onstage. I kept looking down, thinking a clump of white cotton wool would begin poking up. I stuffed it down well before I went onstage, but I never really relaxed when I was doing that solo.

Still, it was wonderful to be alone on the stage with all the lights out, then, suddenly the spotlight turned on. There you are, in the center of the stage with black velvet curtains all around, just standing there in a pool of light in a beautiful long gown.

Two pianos were playing softly in the background, as I recited a monologue about being a shy young English Rose meeting an American GI for the first time. He had given me flowers and a card that read, "Happy Mother's Day." And, I was wondering, "Whatever did he mean?"

It would have been perfect, had it not been for the stuffing. There was a good round of applause after my performance and my mother was thrilled; she loved it.

My mother was in the audience every night and was so happy to see me performing solo on the London stage. That had always been my ambition, my dream—and hers.

At the end of that week though, she told me we were short of money.

"Where did all the money go?" I asked.

"Well, I was buying theater tickets. I came to see you every night," she said.

I couldn't argue with that.

Going to work at the Ambassadors Theatre was a smart move for me. Of course, I was sad to say good-bye to Mr. Murray, and my fiends at the Cabaret Club, who had been so good to me.

Mr. Murray was not at all pleased when I had told him I was leaving. But he had wished me well and told me that he knew Mr. Pemberton and that he was a very fine person to work for. The Ambassadors Theatre was a fine venue, he said.

During the run of the show at Ambassadors, the bombings were increasing, so the performances were put on early in the evenings, from 6 p.m. until 9 p.m.

That schedule allowed people to get to the air raid shelters before the heavy bombings started each night.

Occasionally, the German Air Force would conduct an

early air raid and the theater manager would stop everything and hurry onto the stage and announce the impending danger: "Ladies and gentlemen, the sirens have started— there is an alert. Those that wish to leave may go to the nearest air raid shelters. For those that wish to stay, the show will go on."

A few people would run for the shelter, but most of the audience would stay and see the rest of the show. We all took seriously the statement, "The show must go on." But humor was the real key to our success.

The girls and I used to call Hermione Gingold "Mum." In American lingo that would be "Mom."

The affectionate term was used only between ourselves, and not to her face. The tall, thin, eccentric brunette, who had a soprano voice range and a scissor-sharp wit, didn't look old enough to be our mother of course, although she was about 25 years older than most of us girls.

We'd ask each other, "How's mum tonight?"

"Oh, she's very well," would be the reply.

Or, "She's very scared of the bombings."

Actually Gingold was petrified of the air raids. I can't blame her, having to go on the stage to perform alone with bombs dropping all around; that was frightening.

One night in 1943, Mary, Jackie and myself were due to go on. A heavy raid started. We were determined to begin our comedy routine, but first we had to get down a flight of very narrow stairs in our high heels, to get to the wings.

Gingold was sitting on one of the steps with her head between her hands, crying.

"I can't go on," she sobbed.

We couldn't either, because she was blocking the way down the steps. We felt so sorry for her, but we needed to get onstage.

Finally I said, "Sorry we are going to have to step over you; that's all we can do."

So we did.

The manager was yelling, "Hurry up, you have to get onstage!"

Breathless, we ran out into the spotlight and continued with our sketch. No matter how bad the raids, the show always continued.

As for Gingold, she was a trooper too. She survived the war; in fact, she lived to be almost 90 years old. In the 1950s, she went on to perform in movies, including the Lerner and Loew musical, *Gigi*, with Leslie Caron and Maurice Chevalier.

She sang a duet with Chevalier called, "I Remember it Well." Gingold played Gigi's mum in the movie. For that role, she won a Golden Globe.

She was also a hit on Broadway, and won a Tony Award for best supporting actress in *A Little Night Music*.

Yes, our "mum" did very well for herself. Over the years, she married twice. Her second husband, Eric Maschwitz, was the writer of many much loved songs of the pre-war era including, "These Foolish Things," and "A Nightingale Sang in Berkeley Square." He also wrote the screenplay to *Goodbye, Mr. Chips*.

CHAPTER 17

Lunch With The Generals

G ingold was a wonderful person and certainly a great entertainer. In a *Sweet and Low* production she sported a thoroughly wild Viking costume. We all got a kick out of that.

She could make friends easily—when she wanted to—and was a great friend of Noel Coward. As children, they had attended the Italia Condie Dancing School together in London, as did I for a time.

At one point during the war, she became friendly with the brave and daring U.S. Army Air Force Maj. Gen. James Doolittle.

He was famous for his "Doolittle Raiders." The raiders, all volunteers, flew the first retaliation air raid on Japan in 1942, with a squadron of bombers. Doolittle was a colonel at that time. Some bombers, including Doolittle's, ran out of fuel and crash-landed in China. Most of the crew escaped the Japanese, who at that time were occupying parts of China.

By 1944, Doolittle was promoted to major general, and was in London helping plan the D-Day invasion. But to take his mind off the fighting—at least one would imagine that was so—he came to our show at the Ambassadors Theatre.

One evening during the show, we heard a lot of laughter and applause from one of the boxes. It turned out to be Maj. Gen. Doolittle and his staff, thoroughly enjoying the acts. Afterwards, he said he'd had such a good time that he just had to come backstage to meet Gingold.

Doolittle told the management of the theater that he would like to "pop in" and see the performances whenever he was in London. So he took a box for the run of the show. But he said that on the nights that he wasn't there, if the theater was full and any other soldiers came in looking for seats, they could have his box.

He was good that way; he was a jolly little guy. He became highly decorated and famous for building the morale of the United States military because of his daring Tokyo raid. Keeping up morale is vital in wartime. (Spencer Tracy portrayed Doolittle in the 1944 film, *Thirty Seconds Over Tokyo*. Alec Baldwin played him in the 2001 blockbuster movie *Pearl Harbor*).

During *Sweeter and Lower*, in 1944, a lot of Americans were coming to see us perform. We loved to have them in the audience. The Americans always seemed to enjoy a lively show and I got quite a few fan letters!

Doolittle and Gingold enjoyed each other's company

very much. I guess somewhere in their conversations she let the general know that the food rationing was weakening our dancing abilities.

Although my aunts would send some food items from Grantham when they could, we were still feeling the effects of the lack of enough to eat.

It seemed evident that Doolittle felt quite sorry for us performing on short rations. He told Hermione that he would send a car to the stage door once a month on a Sunday afternoon to take her and the rest of the company down to his house in High Wickham. We would join him for a full, and very delicious, lunch and high tea at the house, which was also his headquarters, he said.

"Then we will see that you are all driven back to the stage door," he assured her.

We only needed to let him know how many were coming so he would know how many cars to send for us. We were all excited about going.

As planned, two unmarked Army cars picked us up and we were off to a very scrumptious steak and potato lunch, and later in the afternoon, a divine high tea.

The general's house was a large, attractive mock Tudor-style home that had been requisitioned during the war for his use, because he was in charge of the United States 8th Army. About six or seven people were living in the house, including two or three colonels.

After lunch, Doolittle would sit around chatting with us about show business. We talked a lot about the theater. One afternoon he told us he used to be a very good acrobat.

We looked at each other in disbelief but tried to humor him.

"Oh yes, I'm sure you were," we all said, smiling at one another.

I think he must have read the disbelief in our eyes. So, the general insisted on proving his claim.

"I'll show you. Move all the chairs back," he commanded, smiling as he took off his jacket.

We moved the chairs out of the way, as he went to the end of the room. Then, after a moment's pause, he did perfect handsprings from one end of the room to the other.

He wasn't very tall, so he was able to move across the room with ease.

We were really quite surprised, and gave him a big round of applause. He looked very pleased with himself. You would've thought he'd just won an Olympic gold medal. In fact, during his lifetime he was awarded far more important medals: the Medal of Honor, the Medal of Freedom, two Distinguished Service Medals, the Silver Star, three Distinguished Flying Crosses, the Bronze Star, and four Air Medals.

Most of the show's cast came regularly each month for the afternoon with the general. We also became good friends with his staff. It was a pleasant relief from our usual schedules.

One wintry afternoon, as soon as we arrived, Doolittle said, "I have a very interesting person coming for lunch."

We were all trying to imagine who it might be. He couldn't keep us in suspense for long.

"I'll tell you who it is. It's General George Patton. He's going to be my guest today."

Patton was one of the 20th Century's greatest warriors and one of the United States' greatest heroes. But things didn't always go the way he wanted, as revealed in the 1970 movie *Patton*, starring George C. Scott.

Doolittle mentioned one problematic incident to us before Patton arrived at the luncheon.

"There's been a bit of scandal in the newspapers about him, but it is very overblown. He is really a very fine person, and a very good friend," Doolittle said.

The scandal involved the reported slapping of a soldier, who Patton apparently thought had behaved cowardly. But it was greatly exaggerated in the press, Doolittle said.

A few minutes later, the guest of honor was ushered in.

I will never forget seeing Gen. George Patton for the first time as he strode into the dining room of the house in High Wickham. It was only a few minutes after we arrived that day. We hardly had time to compose ourselves after the announcement that the famous American general would be joining us.

The tall, ruddy-faced warrior walked in wearing riding britches and carrying his riding crop. I just stared because I had never seen anyone—at least not a general—dressed in jodhpurs before.

Gen. Patton had lunch with us, sitting right across the table from me. He was a very charming companion and I believe that Doolittle was a faithful friend to the beleaguered military giant.

Before being called to London, Patton was engaged in many valiant efforts against the Nazis. He led his army to liberate millions of people in occupied Europe. Patton may have been fierce out on the battlefield, but he was a gentleman when he lunched with us.

Later that day, Doolittle and Patton announced that they had to go into London—we guessed probably for a war meeting.

Perhaps, we thought, they will be talking about the greatest invasion the world had ever known. Because of the huge build up of American forces in England, everyone knew a massive invasion of occupied Europe would happen sooner or later. The Allies would cross the English Channel and arrive on the coast of France, and that would be the beginning of the end of this terrible war. The invasion on June 6, 1944 would later become known as D-Day.

At about six in the evening, it became very, very foggy, making travel back to Cambridge Circus hazardous. The drivers of the cars that were to take us back to the theater came in and announced the bad weather.

"It's really too foggy to drive back to London. So, if it's all right with you, you'll have to spend the night here and we will take you back first thing in the morning," an aide to the general said.

Then it was a case of where would we all sleep?

Fortunately, there was only about six of us visiting on that particular Sunday. Two of the general's male staff said that they would be happy to sleep on the couches, freeing up some beds.

One of the girls was engaged to a colonel there, so we knew where she was going to sleep. That left Jane and me.

"Where are we going to sleep, and can we call our mothers?" we asked.

A telephone was made available right away.

My mother said, "You be sure to sleep with Jane, whatever you do."

When Jane called her mother she was told, "You be sure to sleep with Pauline."

One of the aides came downstairs and told us the only bedroom vacant at the moment was General Doolittle's room.

"He won't be back tonight," the aide said.

"That's fine with us," we replied.

We were taken upstairs to a very large and elegantly decorated bedroom, with a huge bed and a private bathroom. Many large portraits and photographs hung on the walls, and a picture of the general's wife and family was on the dressing table.

We got into bed, but just before we went to sleep, I noticed an armrest coming out of my side of the bed. Embedded in the armrest were two or three telephones and all kinds of switches.

I assumed that if anyone needed to get a hold of Doolittle during the night, they would call him on the phones right next to me.

"What shall I do if the phones start to ring during the night?" I asked Jane.

"I can't very well answer and say, 'This is Pauline, in General Doolittle's bedroom!'"

"If something drastic happens, they will need to call him," Jane said, looking worried.

We started giggling about what we might say and what the consequences might be. I finally decided I wouldn't say anything. I would just let it ring.

Luckily, no phone calls came in during the night and by morning the fog had lifted.

We had a very nice breakfast with *real* eggs and bacon. After breakfast, we had a photo taken of us standing outside the house. Then we were driven back to the stage door of the Ambassadors.

CHAPTER 18

A Prince Comes to Call

Besides the pinup girl routine, our company was also lauded for a sketch called, "Oh Miss Dixie." It was a takeoff of a woman who was famous for her fan dancing, although not as famous or infamous, as Mata Hari was.

We recited:

> Oh Miss Dixie, won't you tell me please,
> How you go onstage and do a tease.

On one occasion we were invited to go over to the Stage Door Canteen, which was in Piccadilly. We were asked to do excerpts from our show on a Sunday evening.

We agreed, and were delighted to find that Bob Hope (that prince of the entertainment world) was also on the program.

It was a successful collaboration and we were later asked to do a repeat performance when Bing Crosby and Noel Coward were performing at the Stage Door Canteen. It was an unforgettable experience to perform for the troops.

At the Ambassadors Theatre we had a "dresser." That's what we called the person who made sure all our changes of costumes were ready when we rushed into the dressing room to change in between acts. Usually, the dressing room was a mess with costumes and dressing gowns hanging here and there.

We had one dresser for the four of us.

She also made sure that all our makeup was lined up at our places on the long dressing table where we sat in a row getting ready. We only had a little bit of room each for our makeup, hairpins, combs and brushes. The dressing table and long mirror were lit by bulbous strip lighting.

We had to buy all our own makeup and keep it in makeup boxes, which were actually tin trays that would help keep things somewhat, tidy. The makeup had to be covered up with a towel to keep it clean, when we went home at night after each show.

Theatrical makeup could be purchased at a shop in Piccadilly. That wasn't too practical, though, because sometimes you had to wait a long time to get the right color lipstick.

I usually bought my supplies from a salesman who would come to the theater, occasionally. He arrived with a suitcase full of lipsticks, eye pencils, powder and blush. I always opted for "Carmen One" or "Carmen Two" red lipstick. It just suited my coloring, fair skin and honey-colored fair hair. My hair became fairer and fairer through the years.

Some of our makeup was quite expensive. It was very heavy makeup because of the footlights and spotlights. We put it on thick, so it would show up under the bright stage lights; otherwise we would look washed out.

Luckily, during the war, makeup wasn't rationed and you could acquire enough to get by with, until the salesman came around again.

When entering our dressing room, you could smell the greasepaint. I relished the smell; it would hit you the minute you walked in.

Of course, when we were filming, the makeup we used was entirely different from the stage makeup. It was all one color, called pancake. Then they would do the eyes and lipstick, but no rouge.

At the Ambassadors, Hermione Gingold had her own dresser, a very nice woman named Kitty, who I believed stayed working for her for most of her theatrical career.

Gingold continued to have friends showing up backstage at the theater. Sometimes they would ask for a date to be arranged and she would oblige.

As we were getting ready to appear onstage one night, Kitty came in and asked if any of the girls would like to go out and have a dinner date with two of Miss Gingold's friends.

"They are Navy men," she said.

I already had a date, so I didn't volunteer. Two other girls said they would like to go out.

The next night, I asked one of them how their date with the sailors went.

"Well, they were very charming. One fellow was blond

and very good-looking. His friend said that he was the prince of Greece, but I don't know if I believe that," she said.

"Why don't you go and ask Hermione," I suggested.

She did, and found out he was!

So, I narrowly missed having a date with Queen Elizabeth II's future husband, Prince Philip. They were wed in 1947, at Westminster Abbey. The fact that I came close to having a date with the prince was something I would remind my own husband, from time to time, during our 50 plus years of married life.

* * *

Like everyone during the war, I had to do a certain amount of war-related work.

Every business building in London had to have three people on the roof every night during the air raids, to put out any fires that might start.

When the sirens sounded, people from each company had to rush up onto the roof of their respective building. They were called firewatchers.

I was paired with a fellow from our theatrical company and also Olive, one of the performers. When our turn came around, we would sleep in the office at the top of the Ambassadors Theatre, to be close to the roof.

I wasn't happy about that, but you do what you have to do when there's war on.

Arrangements were made so bunk beds could be put in one of the offices. Hooks were installed near the office door to hang up our tin helmets. We were required to wear the helmets whenever we were up on the roof.

In the middle of the night, the minute we heard the sirens, we could grab the helmets and run up onto the roof. It was frightening up there. The sirens were going, and you'd hear the boom of the bombs falling and guns in the distance, and here we were standing on the roof.

St. Martin's Theatre was opposite us, right across the alley. They would have people on their roof. We would have people on our roof. We would all wave and yell to each other.

We tried to keep cheerful, but it was terrifying when all the searchlights were scanning the sky and the "ack-ack" guns were firing at the enemy planes.

And to top it all off, my helmet was much too big. It was made for a man. I couldn't wear it. It would fall forward; it would fall backwards. In the end, I just took it off.

We were all dressed in one-piece siren suits that looked a bit like dungarees with sleeves. Actually, they were quite comfortable and very functional.

We had to sleep in the suits on the nights when we were firewatchers, so we could jump out of our bunks and run right up onto the roof, as soon as we heard the siren. Winston Churchill also wore a siren suit throughout most of the war years. He had secret war rooms located far beneath London. But even deep underground, one never knew what weapon might reach you, and you would be lucky to escape with your life. So, it was smart to be already dressed.

Each time our turn came around to be firewatchers, we slept on the bunk beds while waiting to hear the sounds of sirens giving the alarm that London was about to be bombed again.

On the roof we had hatchets, buckets of sand, and buckets of water ready to put out any fires that might start if a bomb fell on us. We would stand there on the theater roof while the raid was going on, and hope and pray they wouldn't hit us.

Sometimes, though, we clowned around a bit, because it would get quite boring if the raid wasn't severe, or if it was focused on the center of London, instead of our area.

Often, the heart of the city would be lit up as bright as day, as thousands of incendiary bombs found their targets.

Other times, when the bombs were pretty close, we would flatten ourselves against the chimney pots and pray that they wouldn't drop an incendiary bomb on our roof.

A huge part of the city was burned in one great big raid. It was absolute chaos with the planes, the fires, and the "ack-ack" guns firing at the Luftwaffe as they flew over London.

One night, I heard that the Windmill Theatre was almost hit. One of the dancers had gone across the road between shows to have a drink in the Red Lion Pub. A bomb fell on the Red Lion and her leg was ripped open.

Another showgirl ran out to help the rescuers who were hurrying to the scene. Behind the pub they had stables with about 18 horses boarded in the stalls there. When the bomb fell hitting part of the pub, the horses made a terrible racket.

The girl, who ran from the Windmill to help, heard the noise in the stables, which had also caught fire. She risked her life, as she drove the horses out of the burning stables all by herself.

The heroine was presented with the St. George Cross for bravery at Buckingham Palace.

While I was doing my fire-watching work, my mother had a habit of sitting at her kitchen window and watching the roof of the Ambassadors Theatre. She could barely see us, but she knew when it was my turn to be up there.

Instead of going down to the nearest shelter, or the underground railway where thousands of people took refuge from the nighttime bombing raids, my mother would watch to make sure nothing happened to me.

Not that she could have prevented anything. But perhaps by watching she felt she could somehow keep me alive.

That is the strength of a mother's love, to risk her own safety by keeping watch over the safety of her child.

CHAPTER 19

Home Is Where the Heart Is

At the end of each year we were allowed to take a week off, with pay. I always went back by train to my aunt's house in Grantham, which is 110 miles north of London.

I packed my clothes in a very smart traveling bag, with my initials embossed on the front. We each had received an initialed traveling bag as a gift from the owners of the Ambassadors Theatre, to show their appreciation for our success with *Sweet and Low*.

It was a gift I prized almost as much as I valued the chance to enjoy the peace and quiet of my birthplace, where I could catch up on my sleep.

Sleep was something we got used to being without. I don't know if I ever had a good night's sleep during the war, except when I was away on holiday.

In May 1943, the RAF's legendary 617 Dam Busters

Squadron, that became known for daring raids over Germany, had a command center in Grantham. They were the aviators who bravely flew over the occupied European continent to destroy the hydroelectric dams near the Ruhr Valley. The Germans were developing heavy water in facilities close to the dams.

We knew that if the Nazis were able to proceed with their experiments, they would be able to build the atom bomb. Developing an atom bomb required heavy water. The English were determined to put a stop to the development.

In the incredibly dangerous raid, led by Guy Gibson, a highly decorated young pilot, the RAF aviators dropped specially designed bombs that bounced along the water until they hit the targeted dams.

The mission succeeded; a major flood ensued. The bomb-making facilities, and other manufacturing plants, were destroyed and that slowed down the Nazi's plan to rule the world. The Dam Busters saved many innocent lives.

One of our pinup girls at the Ambassadors knew the wife of one of these heroes of the dam-busting project, which was kept top secret until the mission was completed. He really knew his business, my friend told me.

They must have had nerves of steel, I thought.

Actor Richard Todd starred in the movie *The Dam Busters*, made in 1954. He lived only a few miles from Grantham.

Another Grantham native, Margaret Thatcher, who now has a hall named after her at a Grantham girls' school and a center named after her at a college in America, wasn't the only other historic person to be connected with my hometown.

Four hundred years before the Dam Busters flew on their dangerous mission, Sir Isaac Newton, the famous scientist, was born just a few miles away in Woolsthorpe; he invented the telescope, discovered gravity and developed calculus. A college is named after him and a statue honoring Newton stands on St. Peter's Hill near the center of my old hometown.

After World War II, the important people of Grantham were featured in a book, called *Highlights of Important People of Grantham*. When the book came out, I was totally surprised to find my picture was included.

I know why Margaret Thatcher and Isaac Newton are in the book—because they are truly famous. But I'm not sure why I'm included.

Things were refreshingly normal in Grantham when I arrived for my short annual holidays. There were really no signs of the "wolves of war" that were terrorizing London. My uncle was still selling petrol and making deals with farmers. The food was plentiful and very good; I ate well.

Air raids were almost unheard of in the town. Usually, raids on rural communities would only happen if a plane was returning to Germany. If the fliers still had an extra bomb or two left over, they would just drop them anywhere.

One night, a single bomb was dropped on the playing fields of a college that was not far from my uncle's garage. It was the only time a bomb fell on my hometown. That was the closest Grantham came to being in an air raid, and it caused quite a stir.

My uncle reacted immediately by getting out his old

hunting riffle. He ran up to the top bedroom, and, taking aim out of the window, he vowed to, "Get as many of them before they ever get into this house. Everybody in this house will go down fighting," he stated.

At that point, I wished I had my kitchen knife with me.

Maybe the reason why the town was not bothered by the nightly Luftwaffe raids was because the Germans didn't know there was a big munitions factory nearby. It was in operation during World War I and probably during WWII as well.

Grantham lies in an out-of-the-way hollow. In the evenings, we would sometimes get a mist over the area and you couldn't see the town very well. I believe that's why they had the munitions factory there. The mist was like a natural camouflage. I am so glad that the town wasn't troubled by the Nazi raiders as much as we were in the capital city.

When I was back in London, as I was walking down the street near the theater one morning, I heard what sounded like trains coming toward me.

I noticed everybody was looking up. In the distance, there was what looked like a swarm of bees, very high up in the sky. I thought it must be planes making all this noise.

All of a sudden, there was complete silence.

Then a few seconds later, there was nothing but the sound of explosions. Everybody on the street where I stood looked at each other, wondering what on earth was happening.

Later that day, Churchill came onto the radio and said that these were jet-propelled, miniature, pilotless planes sent over by remote control. They were called V-1 flying bombs.

As long as we could hear them, we were to look for the

nearest shelter, because the minute they were silent it meant that they were coming down to earth and exploding.

These flying bombs, unfortunately, were all aimed at London.

Our Royal Air Force tried to shoot down a few of them, but not very successfully. The bombs caused the loss of many lives and buildings.

It was only when the RAF could find the launching pads for these pilotless planes on the coast of France, that they were stopped and we had some peace, for a while.

But the worst weapon of the war that the Germans used against us was the V-2 rocket bomb, developed in 1944.

My mother and I were in the shelter one night after we heard the sirens wailing. After a few hours, we waited for the "all clear" to sound. By about six o'clock in the morning, nothing had happened. Finally, at eight o'clock we asked the air raid warden when the "all clear" was going to sound so we could go back to our homes.

"I don't know. I haven't been told anything. I can't see anything flying overhead, or hear any bombing at all. I don't know what's going on," he said.

We decided it must be all right to go home.

Of course, that was the start of the V-2 bombs, delivered by rockets, so they were almost impossible to shoot down. They were being sent over from the coast of occupied France and the damage they did was extensive. One bomb could knock out two buildings wherever it landed.

Unfortunately, these V-2 rocket bombs were moved around on rails or flatbed trucks, sort of like small trains. It was very hard to pinpoint where they were so that the RAF could take out the launching pads.

This dreadful weapon was not destroyed until after V-E Day, that is Victory in Europe Day, May 8, 1945, when the war at last came to an end—at least the war in Europe. The battles in the Pacific lasted a few more months.

Our military finally found the V-2 bases and destroyed them. A V-2 rocket that was captured intact was put on display in Trafalgar Square.

* * *

In the fall of 1944, I had an invitation one night that would change my whole life. A United States Army officer, named Ray Bianucci, came to the stage door at the Ambassadors after the performance, asking to be introduced to me.

The handsome, mustachioed American had a pleasant, persuasive manner and was intent on sweeping me off my feet. He explained that he was a Mickey Radar officer in the United States Army, stationed with the 392nd Bomber Group in Norfolk, England. He asked me out to dinner.

I was ready to refuse, because I didn't know him at all; and I told him so. But he insisted.

"You must remember me from the party at the air force base. You gave a show and we met at the party afterward," said the handsome, smiling officer.

I didn't remember him, but I thought, "Oh, what the heck."

He took me out to dinner. After that, he came to London on leave every chance he got. One evening, we were at dinner in a restaurant.

"Will you marry me, before I go back to the United States?" he suddenly asked me.

"I don't think it's possible," I replied, knowing it had taken other people many months to get paperwork through to marry someone from another country. Red tape was especially long during wartime.

"I'll see what I can do," Ray said.

Fortunately, one of my friends in the show had a pull with one of the generals and they helped to get the paperwork moving. She was actually engaged to a U.S. general at that time and that made a difference. But the wait time to marry was still considerable.

When Ray went back to Norfolk, it was like part of my heart went with him. But I continued my theater work, and the Germans continued their bombing raids on London.

To take our minds off the war, and any absent fiancé, we kept busy by knitting. Millions of other British women were avid knitters as well, probably for the same reasons.

Mary, Jackie and I would sit in the wings and create woolly scarves, mittens or hats; you could volunteer to knit for the allied troops. I knitted scarves for the Russian sailors and some, I believe, also were sent to our own sailors.

The only trouble with our knitting project was that the big balls of khaki-colored wool had some kind of oily grease on them, which left our hands with black marks. It may have been to keep the wool soft. I suppose being in very cold weather at sea, with all that salty air, the knitted scarves and mittens could be weakened. Or, maybe it was a special kind of wool that kept them warmer than the norm. It was more likely that, being in wartime, the wool didn't get washed before it was sold.

We really had no clue; we just kept on knitting. Whatever the cause of the oily substance, we always had to be sure to quickly wash the black grease off our hands before we went onstage.

* * *

Meanwhile, Gingold was still arranging lunches with prominent people. Some of us were invited to lunch with her friend, a Major Scott, on a day when we didn't have to perform in a matinee.

Mary, Jackie and I were quite pleased to go and we got dressed up for the event. We were told that Major Scott would be inviting two friends to join us for lunch at his apartment.

He had a fantastic place on the top floor of a building overlooking Piccadilly. There was a beautiful view of the city from his balcony.

When we arrived, he said that if we wait a few minutes, two friends of his would be arriving as well.

Soon, there was a brisk knock on the door and his aide answered it. In walked David Niven and Broderick Crawford, in uniforms of their respective nations: Great Britain and the United States of America.

We all took one look at them in their uniforms and almost swooned. We could hardly talk. We were overcome by being in the same room with such famous actors. After a few minutes, we were able to speak again.

Niven was a great talker and he soon had us relaxing.

The romantic star of the silver screen had a great sense of humor and kept us in stitches.

When we sat down to lunch, I noticed a little brown capsule beside each place setting.

"These capsules came to me from America," Scott said. "They are vitamin pills. We thought maybe each of you would like to have one."

Well, Mary and Jackie refused because they weren't quite sure what they were going to be like. But, of course, I swallowed my capsule.

David Niven turned to me and said, "From now on I'm going to call you 'Pilly Pauline.' "

The little brown capsule was indeed a vitamin pill, but we didn't have vitamins at that time in England, so it did look strange to us.

I'd never heard of a vitamin pill. I tried it because David Niven was looking at me!

He was a great fellow. He really had a wonderful sense of humor and made you feel at home right away. It did us good to have lunch with him.

And, the "pilly" didn't do me any harm, except that the next day I broke out in red hives. But they soon disappeared.

* * *

By the spring of 1945, the plans that Ray and I had made were progressing. However, getting married to someone from another country—especially someone in the U.S. military— was not so easy. Even with the contacts that we had, Ray and I were experiencing the frustration of being hindered by the reams of red tape, required before we could become man and wife.

Normally, you had to give six months notice while the United States officials looked into your background, if you planned on marrying into the U.S. military.

Fortunately, the strings pulled by one of the girls in the show, did seem to help speed up the process to enable Ray to arrange for me to emigrate from England to the United States. He must have thought that if we weren't married, I wouldn't follow him to America.

It was difficult dating during the war—and nothing like normal dating; it was entirely different. You couldn't spend much time together. Some romances even blossomed in unexpected places, like air raid shelters where people gathered at night.

Couples didn't get a lot of time together. The war saw to that.

Finally, on May 8th, the end of the war was announced. On that day, all the church bells in the kingdom were ringing madly. It was the first time they were rung since the war began. The bells were silenced at the start of the war, because they were only to be rung as a warning, if the invasion actually started.

There was no fear of that any more.

My mother and I went to Trafalgar Square to celebrate. Millions of people had the same idea. Miraculously, Nelson's Column was still standing in the center of the square. After all the bombing, it was incredible to see it still a solid, untouched landmark.

Streamers were flying through the air; the atmosphere was electric. Complete strangers were grabbing each other, kissing each other and hugging. We got pushed around a lot in the huge crowd, especially me being short.

Everyone was singing "Knees Up Mother Brown." Then they sang another song that went:

We're going to hang out our washing on the Siegfried Line.
Have you any dirty washing mother dear?

The Siegfried Line was a German line of defense, near Brandschied, which the American forces had breached on February 4, 1945.

Shortly after the end of the war was announced, the paperwork finally came through allowing Ray and I to marry. We didn't want to wait a minute longer. Only then did I tell my mother about our plans.

She was very upset, of course, that I would be giving up a career I had worked so hard for, and would be going to live in the United States for good. I could understand; she would be left alone.

I could understand her feelings. But as she had lived before in the United States, and loved the country so much, my whole idea was that I could bring her over as soon as people could leave England without too many problems.

She insisted that Ray wasn't right for me and tried everything to deter me from marrying him.

"He's the wrong man for you," my mother told me in no uncertain terms.

But this was one time that her powers of persuasion didn't work.

I told her she could come over and live with us in Naperville, Illinois, or have a home near us. I didn't realize at the time that her heart was not very strong. And there was no way to know then that she would not come again to America. In fact, she passed away just 14 months after I left for the United States.

If I had known her medical condition, I probably would have had second thoughts about leaving home. But she never let on.

* * *

On a June day in 1945, Ray and I were ready to tie the knot. It was very much a war era wedding, with only a handful of people present. Ray had asked some of his friends at his base to come to the wedding; one was to be best man and the others were witnesses.

On the big day, they met my mother and me at the train station at a little village near the base, and presented us with corsages: one for myself, and one for my mother. We rode in a Jeep to the church. I can still picture my mother sitting in the backseat with the officers, getting bumped around as we drove down the narrow, twisty country lane to the church.

She had only met Ray once before the wedding day. Even on that special day, she still didn't want me to get married. That was difficult, but that's the way it was.

In the beautiful little Gothic-style Roman Catholic church we said our vows before a priest from the base. I had never been in a Catholic church before, because we were Protestants.

I didn't make a big fuss for my wedding. I didn't have a long white gown, or veil, or a cadre of bridesmaids. Very few brides did have all the wedding trimmings in those troubled days. The ceremonies were mostly very simple affairs. For my wedding day, I just wore my best dress.

We went through the ceremony, with my mother crying the whole time. Suddenly—with a gold ring on my finger—I realized that I was married.

After the ceremony, we went to a little country hotel, which was about 100 years old. Heavy wooden beams were holding up the whitewashed ceilings.

We had our reception dinner at the hotel. The meal consisted of cold chicken and salad, which was all they could provide, and a very small cake. Afterward, we all went on to the village green outside the hotel and watched people playing bowls for a little while.

Then, the best man offered to take my mother by Jeep back to the train station so she could get home to London. We spent our wedding night in the quaint, old hotel.

The next day, my husband was called back to the base, because they were getting ready to leave for the Pacific. So we went to spend our second night as man and wife in his Nissen hut on the base.

Ray told the five other guys who shared the hut with him to vacate the living space so he could bring his new bride there. They had to find a place to sleep elsewhere that night.

They were good sports about it. But for a joke they put firecrackers under the door and set them off in the middle of the night. It scared the life out of me.

Ray went outside and yelled at them, and they finally stopped their antics. They thought it was very funny.

The following morning, Ray was given a trunk full of papers that were pertaining to the V-2 rocket. His mission was to make sure the trunk was delivered safely to Washington. Wernher von Braun, who developed the V-2 rocket in Germany, had defected to America by that time. The German scientist was retained to help develop rockets for the American space program that eventually propelled humans to the moon.

Within a few years, twelve Americans were to make very dramatic marks on history by walking on the lunar surface.

So, on the third day of our marriage, Ray set sail for the United States. I took the train back to London, a married woman, quite upset that my husband had to leave me so soon.

CHAPTER 20

Biding My Time

S o now I was married and ready to go for a second time to America, where I would join my husband. As soon as he was discharged from the military, we would set up house near Chicago—he promised me that.

I couldn't wait.

Unfortunately, I would have to wait several months for my sailing orders!

The tens of thousands of war brides were told that five or six ships were waiting to take the spouses of United States servicemen across the Atlantic Ocean to the "New World." We were told we would get our sailing orders soon to leave for a new life in a new country. The intense excitement we felt about leaving was short-lived when we realized that it would take longer than we thought.

It was also unfortunate that I had already turned in my

notice at the Ambassadors, because I expected to sail almost within a few weeks of getting married.

My last two weeks in *Sweeter and Lower* meant training someone to take my place.

Before I left, the girls and staff presented me with a beautiful antique set of hairbrushes and combs, all made of silver.

It was difficult to buy gifts like that during the war, except in pawnshops. One of the girls found the set and knew it would be perfect for a new bride; I was delighted. She told me that Gingold contributed heavily to the gift.

I was also presented with a signed photograph from Gingold, and photographs of the *Sweeter and Lower* cast dressed in costume, which I still have in my personal collection; I treasure them all. The photographs, which once hung in the theater foyer, show us posing in our exotic outfits.

As the weeks went by, no sailing orders came, and I began to get very worried. I had no job; things were getting quite tough.

I went back to stay with my mother. I still had an agent, and one morning he called me and asked if I had ever been a stand-in.

I never had considered doing that, "But there's always a first time," I said.

He advised me to go down to a film studio where a selection was being made for a stand-in for Glynis Johns, a well-known film actress. She was one year younger than me, and was quite famous in England at that time. She had appeared in many well-produced movies.

"Johns has the same coloring as you," my agent said. "She is looking for a stand-in for her latest film. Just go and stand beside her. With the right lighting—you never know—you could be her stand-in," he surmised.

I thought, "Well it's something to do."

But believe it or not, when I got there I saw that we did have the same type of complexion, height and hair color; we looked almost identical.

I was warned ahead of time that she could be a reserved type of person sometimes. So I kept out of her way, and said little. It worked. I was hired. We got along fine.

I had one major disappointment during the filming. In one scene, Glynis Johns was supposed to be dressed in a beautiful, white evening gown. I was looking forward to being dressed like that when I stood in for her, while the technicians worked on getting the correct lighting.

As the stand-in, I was to walk across the set several times in a similar stunning, long white evening gown, so they could get the lighting just right, before filming the scene.

But when it came time for me to do that, and get a lovely evening gown to wear in the scene, the studio had run out of coupons. Even film companies needed coupons at that time to buy clothes.

"Can't you get yourself a pretty white nightgown?" the director asked.

So that's what I ended up doing. It was very embarrassing being photographed at all angles in a nightgown as I walked across the room, moving here and there, mimicking every action the star was to make in that scene.

When they were ready to shoot, I had to step aside and that would be it for my part. It was tedious in a way, because you could stand there for 15 minutes while the technicians tried to get the lighting just right, knowing that in the final version, you would be nowhere to be seen.

But the studio paid pretty well, so at least there was money coming in.

That film was shown in the United States and Great Britain. It was a wartime movie. Glynis Johns' character was in the Auxiliary Territorial Service, a branch of the English Army, and had to wear a uniform in some scenes, of course.

When I stood in for Johns for a scene requiring a uniform, we had plenty of coupons for that outfit. Too bad they ran out before the glamorous evening gown scene.

My stand-in duties also included bringing the movie star a cup of tea when she wanted one, and little helpful things like that.

Meanwhile, my mother had been in conversation with the agent, and the conversation had turned to horses.

"Can Pauline ride? Is she good with horses?" the agent asked.

"Oh yes," my mother assured him without hesitation.

As the filming progressed, there was talk of going on location, and one day the assistant director came over to me and laid out the schedule.

"We are going to be going on location and you'll be coming along," he told me.

"Oh that's great," I said, hoping it was somewhere warm and sunny.

"We're going into the countryside. But Glynis won't be coming," he said. "You'll be doubling for her."

"Well, what will I be doing?" I asked him.

"You'll be on a horse. You'll be racing along and you'll have to jump off, before it crashes into something," he said.

I went very pale and just stared at him. I hadn't been on a horse since I was 12 years old.

"Oh well … great," I said, trying to sound positive.

Then I went home and raised Cain with my mother.

"Did you tell my agent I could ride a horse?" I demanded.

She thought there would be no problem.

"If you've ridden a horse, you never forget," she said.

"Don't be silly. I won't get on a big horse and jump off while it's galloping along," I protested.

My mother persisted.

"Don't you remember, when you were 12 years old, you used to ride around on ponies at the seaside?"

"This is *not* exactly the same thing. If you want to lose a daughter this is a good way to go about it," I stated. "I couldn't possibly jump off a horse that's galloping at full speed."

That night I tossed and turned wondering how I could get out of the horse stunt.

The next day, I went to the assistant director and told him I was very sorry, but I had received my sailing orders to leave for the United States—which was not true. I wished it were true.

"I won't be able to go on with the stand-in work," I said.

Then I approached Miss Johns to tell her that I was sorry, but I could not stand in for her anymore.

When she heard I was going to the United States, she asked me if I thought I would like it there.

"Oh, I've been there before," I said. "I worked in Hollywood, and I went to school with Judy Garland. I did promotional work on the radio, and was in films before the war."

Although Johns had made movies in England, filming in America was a very big deal. Hollywood was the ultimate destination for many actors and actresses.

She started questioning me about the studios and everything about making movies over there. We had tea together and chatted like we'd never chatted before.

Until then, we'd gotten along well, but she was someone I never tried to be really friendly with. Suddenly we were best friends.

Johns eventually made it to America. She played a mermaid in *Miranda*. She played opposite Danny Kay in the film, *The Court Jester*, and also eventually appeared in *A Little Night Music*, with Hermione Gingold, on Broadway.

CHAPTER 21

War Brides Ahoy!

Those seven months of waiting for sailing orders were the longest months of my life.

At last, we got word that the United States government agreed to pay for the passage of all the war brides to join their husbands in New York. An act of Congress approved the expenses for the approximately 70,000 war brides.

With the funding approved, the government was able to requisition none other than the *Queen Mary*, and other ships that became available to transport us.

Finally, in January 1946, I got a postcard in the mail informing me that I would be sailing on a converted Red Cross ship. It sounded pretty good to me. I was to be on the very first WWII war brides ship to set sail from England; it was called SS *Argentina*.

I never thought I would get passage on the first war

brides ship. Our vessel sounded solid. It had traveled the world during the war. Ports of call included Australia, India and Casablanca. I was just glad I wouldn't be on the *Queen Mary*.

Our orders were clear. We had to go down to an encampment and stay there for two or three days before we could board the ship. We had to have physical examinations and produce a certificate from our doctors saying we were in good physical shape. We also had to show letters from our former employers stating we were of good character.

Eventually, I boarded the SS *Argentina* in Southampton on January 26th, as the mayor of the town and many friends and relatives waved us *bon voyage*. We sailed out of Southampton en route to New York and into some very choppy waters. The North Atlantic in January and February is no picnic, and my old friend, seasickness, was with me again.

I shared a cabin with three other brides. They didn't suffer from the ship's motion as much as I did; as usual, I couldn't keep anything down.

The voyage was absolutely awful. Normally, they don't send people over from England to the United States during the months of January and February because of the wintry weather.

We went through a horrible storm from the day we left, until the day we arrived in New York. It was a rough experience all the way that I will never forget. There was turmoil inside and outside of the ship.

Some of the pregnant brides suffered miscarriages. It was tragic to hear them tell us about losing their babies.

Some of the women, who had brought little babies with

them, would have to put them down in the ship's corridors if they suddenly became drastically ill with seasickness. Babies were all over the place; the journey became known as "The Diaper Run." All the disposable nappies were used up long before the nine-day trip ended.

I just tried to keep my thoughts on Ray. Before we met, Ray had sustained an injury. It happened somewhere over Germany during a flight to identify some equipment problems in the bombers.

They were having some trouble with the northern bombsite on the planes. The bombsite is a locator on the lead plane and is used to look at the bomb target site so pilots can know that they are over the correct location. Then they would relay where they were to the rest of the bomber squadron.

Ray was responsible for putting the northern bombsite on the lead plane. To find out what the problem was, one of the captains made a suggestion.

"Why don't you come on board the plane on a raid with us, and you can look at it and see what the problem is?" he asked Ray.

Although he wasn't supposed to fly on the raids, Ray went along. While they were in flight, he was walking along the aisle in the middle of the plane, when he slipped and fell halfway through the bomb bay door.

He found himself hanging on, but his leg went through and got twisted. The crew hauled him back up into the plane.

He should have been hospitalized. But they wrapped up his leg, and he kept on working, because they didn't have any replacement for Mickey Radar personnel.

Eventually, after the war, he had two operations on his leg. The operations were performed between tours of duty while he was a project officer, on the development of the United States' first "pilotless" plane.

But he walked with a slight limp for the rest of his life.

As we war brides continued our treacherous, nine-day voyage across the Atlantic, I was confined to my cabin and subsisted on dried crackers and tea.

The three other women that shared my cabin decided that maybe I would be better up on deck, getting some fresh Atlantic Ocean air.

So between them, they managed to haul me up onto the deck. They put me in a deck chair and wrapped me in some blankets and hoped that the sea air would do me some good.

The only problem was that they forgot that I was up there! And the storm became even more intense.

"Batten down the hatches," the captain ordered, meaning close up all the doors tightly; and nobody would be allowed up on deck.

Eventually, one of my cabin mates suddenly remembered where I was. She dashed along to see the captain and explained that one of the war brides was still up on deck.

They sent some sailors out there to find me on the heaving, rain-spattered deck.

I was absolutely frozen.

The whole time that the storm was raging, and I was up on the deck, I was praying that the next big wave would wash me overboard and I would not have to suffer anymore.

When I got back down to the cabin, they had to thaw me out first. Then, it was back to tea and crackers again.

I lost at least four pounds before I arrived in America, where a big welcome party was planned for us at a grand New York hotel. That's where the officials would bring the brides, and they would meet their husbands at the hotel.

On the dockside, the mayor of New York was there and the bands were playing.

Then, to my utter surprise, I saw that my husband had managed to sneak onto the dock, and he was there, standing at the bottom of the gangplank to welcome me. For a moment, I thought I must have been dreaming.

When I realized he was really there waiting for me, that's when I knew that all the stormy weather I had endured in my life until then was worthwhile.

Ray just couldn't wait for me to get to the hotel as all the husbands were ordered to do, and wait for their brides. None of the husbands were supposed to be at dockside. But my husband was never one who liked to take orders.

Consequently, all the newsmen that were hovering around immediately grabbed their cameras and took pictures of us together.

That's how Ray and I came to be photographed the minute I stepped off the ship, and we appeared in all the New York newspapers the next day.

The spotlight had found me again.

The End

CPSIA information can be obtained
at www.ICGtesting.com
Printed in the USA
FFOW03n2302260415
12934FF